D1267835

England and Italy
1859–60

England and Italy
1859–60

DEREK BEALES

Thomas Nelson and Sons Ltd
London Edinburgh Paris Melbourne Johannesburg
Toronto and New York

THOMAS NELSON AND SONS LTD
Parkside Works Edinburgh 9
36 Park Street London W1
312 Flinders Street Melbourne C1

302–304 Barclays Bank Building
Commissioner and Kruis Streets
Johannesburg

THOMAS NELSON AND SONS (CANADA) LTD
91–93 Wellington Street West   Toronto 1

THOMAS NELSON AND SONS
18 East 41st Street New York 17 N.Y.

SOCIÉTÉ FRANÇAISE D'ÉDITIONS NELSON
97 rue Monge Paris 5

———

Preface

I KNOW of three monographs whose scope is similar to that of this book : H. Ley's *Die italienische Einigung und die englische Politik, 1859–61* ; A. Signoretti's *Italia e Inghilterra durante il Risorgimento* ; and M. B. Urban's *British Opinion and Policy on the Unification of Italy, 1856–61*. There are, in addition, many short surveys of the subject, of which the best are to be found in R. W. Seton-Watson's *Britain in Europe, 1789–1914* and in H. W. V. Temperley and L. M. Penson's *Foundations of British Foreign Policy*. There are three excellent articles dealing with particular episodes : Dr H. Hearder's on Malmesbury's policy before the outbreak of the Franco-Austrian War (*Rassegna storica del Risorgimento*, vol. xliii), Mr A. J. P. Taylor's on the diplomatic background of the Villafranca agreement (*English Historical Review*, vol. li), and Professoressa M. Avetta's on 'the Lacaita incident' (*Rassegna storica del Risorgimento*, vol. xxi (i)). Numerous other historical studies, of which probably the most influential have been Dr G. M. Trevelyan's volumes on *Garibaldi*, treat more or less fully questions which this book also attempts to answer. It will be apparent from the footnotes and the Bibliography that I have relied heavily on the large literature which the subject has attracted.

The principal justification for reconsidering these questions is that most of the writers in this field have lacked some of the most important material. None of the monographs and few of the other works use the private papers of Queen Victoria, Palmerston, Gladstone and Cowley ; the Russell papers, though better known, have not been thoroughly exploited ; and the same applies, at least in England, to the modern editions of Cavour's correspondence and Massari's diary, and to other fruits of recent Italian historical scholarship. For this period, only two authors—H. C. F. Bell, in his *Lord Palmerston*, and W. E. Mosse, in his *The European Powers and the German*

Question, 1848–71—have used these English documents extensively. Neither of these books devotes much space to the Italian crisis. Only Mr D. Mack Smith among English historians has taken advantage of the Italian work, in his *Cavour and Garibaldi, 1860*. There would seem therefore to be room for a fresh study of the subject.

I have to acknowledge the gracious permission of Her Majesty the Queen to use material from the Royal Archives, Windsor Castle. The late Countess Mountbatten of Burma kindly allowed me to see some of the Palmerston papers.

I have received a great deal of help, advice and encouragement, especially from Mr Mack Smith, the Master of Sidney and Dr O. O. G. M. MacDonagh. This book has also benefited from the criticisms of the Master of Peterhouse, Dr G. S. R. Kitson Clark, Dr D. F. Mackay and Sir Charles Webster. Professor A. M. Ghisalberti, Professor W. Maturi and Professoressa E. Morelli advised me on my work in Italy. Professor L. Bulferetti and Professor S. Mastellone supplied me with important material. Dr A. C. de Breycha-Vauthier, Professor A. Briggs, Dr G. R. Elton, Dr R. Robson and Dr Trevelyan drew my attention to sources which otherwise I should have missed. Many archivists have taken much trouble to assist me, in particular Mr N. Blakiston, Mrs G. Blois and Dr D. E. Rhodes. I was enabled to pay two visits to Italy by a grant from the Worts Fund of the University of Cambridge and through the benefaction of Mr R. E. Hentsch. Finally I should like to acknowledge my great debt to the Master and Fellows of Sidney Sussex College for their generous support while I have been preparing this book. To all who have helped me I am most grateful, and I am sorry that this book is not a better witness to their kindness.

D. E. D. B.

Sidney Sussex College,
Cambridge.
15 July 1960

Acknowledgments

Thanks are due and are hereby rendered to the Earl of Clarendon for permission to quote from the Clarendon Papers, and to the following publishers for permission to quote from copyright works : Messrs Edward Arnold (Publishers) Ltd. for *The Life and Letters of the Fourth Earl of Clarendon* by Sir H. E. Maxwell; Messrs Ernest Benn Ltd. for *Life of Richard Cobden* by J. Morley ; Cambridge University Press for *Foundations of British Foreign Policy* edited by H. W. V. Temperley and L. M. Penson ; Messrs J. M. Dent & Sons Ltd. for *Life of Mazzini* by Bolton King ; Messrs Eyre & Spottiswoode (Publishers) Ltd. for *The Paris Embassy during the Second Empire* by the Hon. F. A. Wellesley ; Nicola Zanichelli editore, Bologna, for *Cavour e l'Inghilterra*, carteggio con V. E. d'Azeglio a cura della Reale Commissione Editrice dei carteggi cavouriani and for *Il carteggio Cavour-Nigra dal 1858 al 1861* a cura della Reale Commissione Editrice dei carteggi cavouriani ; Messrs Victor Gollancz Ltd. for *Gladstone and Palmerston* by P. Guedalla ; Messrs Hamish Hamilton Ltd. for *The Trouble-Makers* by A. J. P. Taylor ; Messrs Longmans, Green & Co Ltd. for *Clio, A Muse and Other Essays* by G. M. Trevelyan, for *The Later Correspondence of Lord John Russell*, edited by G. P. Gooch, and for *The Life of 2nd Earl Granville* by Lord Edmond Fitzmaurice ; Messrs Macmillan & Co Ltd. for *The Life of William Ewart Gladstone* by J. Morley ; Messrs John Murray (Publishers) Ltd. for *The Letters of Queen Victoria* edited by A. C. Benson and Viscount Esher, for *Letters of the Prince Consort* edited by K. Jagow, for *A Memoir of Sidney Herbert* by Lord Stanmore, and for *The Life of Benjamin Disraeli* by W. F. Monypenny and G. E. Buckle ; and Oxford University Press for *Early Victorian England* edited by G. M. Young.

Note

The following abbreviations have been used in the footnotes :

RA	Royal Archives, Windsor Castle
BMS	Palmerston Papers, Broadlands
RP	Russell Papers
CP	Cowley Papers
GP	Gladstone Papers
PRO	Public Record Office
BM	British Museum
F.O.	Foreign Office Papers, Public Record Office
CC Ing.	*Cavour e l'Inghilterra*
QVL	*Letters of Queen Victoria*

Where a document which I have seen in manuscript is also available in print, I have quoted—or referred to—the published version unless there is a special reason (such as defective transcription or dating) for quoting or referring to the original. For example, I have referred to the Foreign Office Papers only in default of the Blue Books.

When an original has been quoted, I have tried to reproduce the spelling and punctuation exactly.

The Palmerston Papers appear to be uncatalogued, and so no more than a date reference can be given to them.

Contents

TO

MY FATHER AND MOTHER

Introduction

IN the spring of 1859 Italy still contained six sizable independent states, and in addition Lombardy and Venetia formed part of the Austrian Empire. By the spring of 1861 virtually the whole peninsula, except Venetia and a much shrunken Papal State, had been united under King Victor Emanuel of Piedmont-Sardinia. The unification of Italy amounted to a drastic remodelling of the European state-system ; and the entire two years were one long international crisis, during which a general war might have broken out at almost any moment.

The Italian crisis has a specially prominent place in English history, on three main counts. First, England is commonly believed to have favoured unification, at least after June 1859, when the Whig-Liberal Ministry of Lord Palmerston succeeded the Conservative Ministry of Lord Derby ; and this is usually regarded as the cardinal instance of her official sympathy with European nationalism. So the episode ranks as one of the most significant in the history of her foreign policy. Second, the making of English policy in this crisis was a peculiarly difficult task, because the mid-Victorian public took a lively interest in foreign, and particularly in Italian, affairs, and because the Court and the principal Liberal Ministers were at loggerheads about them. This is therefore a *locus classicus* for students of 'foreign policy and the democratic process'. Third, certain historians have claimed that England's Italian policy was the crucial issue in the General Election of 1859 and the subsequent Parliamentary struggle : that—to state it crudely—the change of Government occurred because the

Conservatives were ' anti-Italian ' while the people and the Liberals were ' pro-Italian '. If so, the occasion is one of the few when external factors have decisively affected the course of English domestic politics.

The object of this book is to consider the English reaction to the Italian crisis in such a way as to answer three questions : what, and especially how ' pro-Italian ', was England's policy ? how was it arrived at ? and what was the importance of England's Italian policy as an issue in the domestic political crisis of 1859 ?

No attempt is made to estimate the effectiveness of England's policy, except, very generally, in the Conclusion. This book is concerned with her intentions. Public opinion and internal politics are treated, except during the political crisis, only in so far as they affected foreign policy.

In Chapter I the Italian background and the story of the two critical years are briefly sketched, and in Chapter II the English background. Thereafter the treatment is chronological.

Chapter I

Italian Unification

ALTHOUGH Italy had been politically divided in one way or another for about fourteen centuries, the particular division existing in 1859 dated back, apart from minor modifications, to the Treaty of Vienna of 1815. The great object of that Treaty, concluded after the final overthrow of the Empire of Napoleon I, was to secure Europe against a revival of French imperialism. In Italy, with that end in view, Piedmont was strengthened, and Austria was confirmed in her possession of Lombardy and Venetia. At that time few even among Italians advocated the unification of Italy, and the parties to the Treaty, especially Austria, were strongly opposed to it.

Between 1815 and 1848 important sections of the population in all the Italian states came to feel a need for Liberal internal reforms, and numerous attempts were made to persuade the various rulers to grant them. But Austria dominated the peninsula, and she used her power to buttress the other Governments in their refusal to make any concessions whatever. So the removal of Austrian influence from Italy was really an indispensable preliminary even to local reforms. As yet this conclusion was not widely accepted. But there was a small party of republican fanatics, led by Giuseppe Mazzini from the 1830s onwards, who not only accepted it, but went a stage further both in theory and in practice, and worked for a national revolution to expel Austria and unite Italy. It was they who planned most of the frequent but petty risings of this period. Liberals dreaded Revolution ; but the logic of

I

Italy at the beginning of 1859

their situation, as they slowly came to appreciate it, impelled them also towards extremism.

In 1848, while Austria was distracted by domestic troubles, a series of revolts overturned the old order in Italy, and throughout most of Europe. Some of the Italian rulers fled at once. Others granted Liberal constitutions, only to be driven out shortly afterwards by republicans. But Austria soon recovered, and Reaction triumphed over the whole Continent. In Italy all the exiled sovereigns had been restored and almost every concession had been repudiated before the close of 1849. Piedmont, the one state which defied this pattern, fought two campaigns against Austria in support of Lombard revolts, was totally defeated, and retained her constitution.

It was now scarcely possible for Italians to doubt that Austria was the arch-enemy of all reform in the peninsula. But it was very difficult to see how she was to be outmatched. The Piedmontese army had been no more successful against her than Revolution had been. Plainly the Italians could not free themselves. Their best hope lay in gaining, through the agency of Piedmont, the alliance of a Great Power strong enough to defeat Austria in war.

The prestige of Piedmont as the only constitutional Italian state grew steadily between 1849 and 1859, while the Mazzinians' declined, both in Italy and outside. Count Cavour, Prime Minister of Piedmont from 1852 onwards, made her hitherto backward system of government more respectable by Liberal reforms. Many prominent Liberals from other parts of Italy took refuge in Piedmont, and more announced their willingness to follow her lead. She joined the Western Powers against Russia in the middle of the Crimean War, in 1855, and a year later helped to procure the discussion of ' the Italian Question ' during the peace Congress at Paris. Cavour wrote in 1857 :

Events have led Piedmont to take up a definite and firm position in Italy. This position is not without dangers, I know, and I feel the full weight of the responsibility that thus falls on me. But it was forced upon us by honour and duty. Since Providence has willed that Piedmont alone in Italy should be free and independent, Piedmont must use her freedom and independence to plead before Europe the cause of the unhappy peninsula. We will not shrink from this perilous task. The King, the people, are determined to carry it through to the end.[1]

In fact, many Piedmontese thought in terms of the aggrandisement of their own state rather than of the emancipation of Italy. But the two potentially conflicting aims did not make for different policies at this stage. A successful war against Austria was the necessary first step in each case.

Piedmont was enabled to perform ' this perilous task ' by the Emperor Napoleon III of France. A revolutionary in his youth, he had a streak of genuine nationalist idealism. He was also anxious for an opportunity to upset the settlement of 1815 and defeat Austria, his country's traditional enemy. Only by fighting a victorious war could he live up to his great name. After an attempt on his life by an Italian exile, Felice Orsini, in January 1858, he became active in the Italian cause. It was a favourable moment, since Austria, having disappointed both sides by her neutrality in the Crimean War, was still diplomatically somewhat isolated. Meeting at Plombières on 21 July 1858, Napoleon and Cavour agreed to provoke a war against her and to try to drive her from Italy. The report of their conversation sent by Cavour to his King lays bare the plot :

The Emperor began by saying that he was determined to support Sardinia with all his strength in a war against Austria, provided that the war should be undertaken for a non-revolutionary cause which could be justified in the eyes of diplomacy and still more of public opinion in France and Europe.[2]

[1] 21 June, to Contessa di Circourt (*CC Ing.*, vol. ii, part ii, p. 253)
[2] 24 July : *Il Carteggio Cavour-Nigra dal 1858 al 1861* (Bologna, 1926-9), vol. i, p. 103

A good pretext was difficult to find. The most promising seemed to be the chronic discontent in the Duchy of Modena, which could probably be fomented to the point when the Duke would put himself in the wrong by insulting Piedmont and summoning Austria to his aid. France would then intervene as Piedmont's ally.

Turning next to examine the means of ensuring a happy issue out of the war, the Emperor observed that we must try to isolate Austria and to deal only with her ; hence his great concern that the war should be motivated by a cause which would not alarm the other Powers and which would be popular in England. The Emperor seemed convinced that the one we had adopted answered this double purpose. The Emperor is absolutely confident of the neutrality of England ; he recommended us to make every effort to influence public opinion in that country to force her Government, which is its slave, to undertake nothing in favour of Austria. He relies equally on the Prince of Prussia's antipathy to the Austrians to keep Prussia from pronouncing against us. As for Russia, he has the Emperor Alexander's formal promise, several times repeated, not to oppose his designs on Italy. If the Emperor is not deceiving himself—and I am rather inclined to believe he is not from all he has told me—the question would be restricted to a war between France and us on one side and Austria on the other.[1]

If France and Piedmont should be victorious, Lombardy and Venetia were to be annexed to Piedmont. With the removal of the influence of Austria, her satellites would be fatally weakened, and Piedmont could expect further gains in the North—probably Modena and Parma, and certainly the Romagna, a part of the Papal State. There might also be erected a Central Italian Kingdom based on Tuscany. The Pope was to be left in possession at least of the City of Rome ; the King of Naples would remain undisturbed. If all went

[1] 24 July : *Carteggio Cavour-Nigra*, vol. i, pp. 106–07

well, the resulting four states would be federated under the presidency of the Pope. France was to receive Savoy and perhaps Nice from Piedmont; and Prince Napoleon, the Emperor's cousin, was to marry Princess Clotilde, Victor Emanuel's daughter.

This was the plot which caused the Italian crisis of 1859–61, and so led to the unification of Italy. But that was not the object of the plot. Although Cavour pointed out to King Victor Emanuel that Piedmont would effectively control the peninsula under the terms of Plombières, there was no hint that Italy might soon be politically integrated. Napoleon intended a federation; he could not wish to help establish a powerful new state on his frontier. Unification remained for many Italians the ultimate goal. But practical expectation stopped short at the expulsion of Austria, the aggrandisement of Piedmont and the remodelling of the northern states.

Nor was it, on the surface at least, a plot to liberate Italy. No provision was made for reform in the territories to be freed. The Italian Question seemed to have been reduced to a problem in pure *Realpolitik*. Many people feared that eventually Piedmont would find she had merely helped to substitute French for Austrian despotism in Italy. It was a risk Cavour had to take. A Liberal policy, as he said, had to be a national policy; and only the French alliance could make a national policy practicable. Perhaps he was right too in believing that his was the last chance to pursue a policy at once national and Liberal.

National sentiment in Italy [he said] is stronger than Liberal opinion : if tomorrow a despot, the King of Naples, raises the national standard and makes war on the Austrians, that despot will be even more popular than constitutional Piedmont. England may be sure of this : today in Italy it is Piedmont which confronts

Austria ; if Piedmont falls tomorrow, her place will be taken by the Revolution.[1]

His gamble was successful, and beyond his hopes : Italy was unified and still Liberal in 1861. The crisis divides naturally into three phases, as first North, then Central and last South Italy was in dispute. Austria was duly goaded into aggression in April 1859, though not by the exploitation of discontent in the Duchy of Modena ; she was defeated by France and Piedmont ; and yet she remained isolated until the end of June. Napoleon's calculations had to this point proved remarkably accurate. Then, early in July, largely because Prussia threatened to upset them by intervening on the side of Austria, he suddenly made peace at Villafranca, near Verona, before his army had conquered Venetia. Piedmont was allowed to annex Lombardy, but for some months afterwards it seemed likely that the old state-system of Central Italy, overthrown during the war, would be restored. Cavour had left office in despair ; Napoleon was bound by the peace not to obstruct the return of the rulers who had fled. Gradually the tense situation changed. The revolutionary Governments of Central Italy succeeded in maintaining themselves, and the peoples declared for annexation to Piedmont. Austria dared not try aggression a second time ; France and England aligned themselves against her. Cavour was recalled to power in January 1860, and in March Piedmont annexed Central Italy while Napoleon took his reward of Savoy and Nice. The situation might now have been stabilised. But in May Giuseppe Garibaldi, already famous as a guerrilla commander, was persuaded to lead an expedition to Sicily. Against all odds he gained control of the island, and then of Naples, and in November he handed over his conquests to King Victor

[1] 11 October 1858 : G. Massari, *Diario dalle cento voci 1858–60* (Bologna, 1959), p. 47

Emanuel. The last official armed resistance ceased in February 1861.

The unification of Italy was by far the greatest territorial change in Europe since the Treaty of Vienna. It was also probably the most striking of the successes of nineteenth-century nationalism. A new Great Power had been created. The manner of the achievement was as remarkable as the achievement itself. Garibaldi's banditry was even more brilliant than the *Realpolitik* of Napoleon and Cavour. But good luck played a principal part. At the beginning of 1859 the international situation was exceptionally favourable. That it never deteriorated to the point when the Northern Powers would intervene to prevent the unification of Italy was largely because no-one could foresee the actual course of unification. For none of the participants governed the process; none could have united Italy by himself; and none wholeheartedly welcomed the result. Garibaldi bitterly resented the use made by Piedmont of his victories; Mazzini, though he had advocated unification for thirty years, hated the monarchy which gained by it; Cavour may have aimed at it in the long run, but he did his best to stop Garibaldi's decisive expedition and would have preferred to wait a while before incorporating Naples and Sicily; Napoleon III did not desire it, but by fighting Austria set it in train; and many Liberals who had intended merely to obtain reforms in their own particular states found that in the event they were promoting the nationalist cause. It was only by the interaction and opposition of half-blind forces that unification triumphed.

Chapter II

The English Background

I

FOREIGN affairs had a remarkable fascination for the mid-Victorians. G. M. Young wrote :

From 1815 to the Revolution of '48 foreign affairs had engaged but a small share of the public attention. . . . But from 1850 onwards the focus of interest is overseas ; the soldier, the emigrant, and the explorer, the plots of Napoleon III and the red shirt of Garibaldi, take and fill the imagination.[1]

Almost every year between 1848 and 1865 some external question stirred English feeling deeply, often to the extent of inducing a crisis in home politics. The principal episodes deserve brief description.[2]

The 1848 Revolutions naturally aroused intense interest. The Reaction aroused even more. In particular, the subjugation of Hungary by the Russians and Austrians was followed by such unnecessarily severe treatment of the rebels that Louis Kossuth, the Hungarian national leader, became a hero—and General Haynau, 'the Austrian Butcher', a villain—in the eyes of Englishmen. When Haynau came to London in 1850 he was frequently insulted and several times physically attacked; when Kossuth came in 1851 he was given a royal reception all

---

[1] ed. G. M. Young, *Early Victorian England* (London, 1934), vol. ii, p. 482
[2] For a list of Ministries and Ministers see Appendix. For a list of the general authorities for this section see Bibliography, section VI B.

over the country. On both occasions there was a political crisis at Cabinet level, since Lord Palmerston, the Liberal Foreign Secretary, was only with difficulty restrained from openly adopting the public's views.

Palmerston had been in office for most of forty-three years, and Foreign Secretary for most of twenty, before he made his great popular reputation early in 1850 in the unworthy cause of Don Pacifico. Pacifico was a Portuguese Jew resident in Greece who, having been born in Gibraltar, claimed to be a British citizen. As such he made an exorbitant demand for compensation from the Greek Government for damage done to his shop by an Athenian mob. Palmerston supported him to the limit. Regardless of the risk he was running of provoking a European war, he sent off a naval squadron, which blockaded Greece until she paid up. The House of Lords then passed a vote of censure on the Liberal Government, mainly because of Palmerston's behaviour in the Pacifico case. But the House of Commons upheld Palmerston. This was the first clear demonstration of Members' admiration for him and their liking for an assertive foreign policy, sentiments which the public was found to share.

Another English political crisis was touched off by the French *coup d'état* of 2 December 1851, when the future Emperor Napoleon III overthrew the Second Republic. This further victory for Reaction precipitated an invasion panic in England. Palmerston this time found himself on the unpopular side, since he had expressed approval of the *coup* ; and, because the Cabinet had not authorised his action, he was dismissed. Without him, however, the Liberal Ministry was hopelessly weak, and it fell in February 1852.

Two years later public opinion forced the country into the Crimean War. But operations went badly, and in February 1855 the Government of Lord Aberdeen was brought down, having refused to institute an inquiry into the whole conduct of the war. Palmerston had made himself the symbol of patriotism and Russophobia. It became necessary to make him Prime Minister, despite the fact that the official leader of the Liberals was Lord John Russell, who had been Prime Minister from 1846 to 1852.

During Palmerston's Premiership, which lasted (with one intermission of sixteen months in 1858-9) until his death in 1865, foreign affairs continued to excite public feeling and to affect domestic politics. In February 1857 the Government was defeated in the House of Commons because it had made war on China ; Palmerston dissolved Parliament, and won the election. Later in the same year the Indian Mutiny stunned and horrified English opinion. Orsini's attempt to assassinate Napoleon III led to the fall of Palmerston's Ministry in February 1858 : the plot had been hatched in England, and the Government wished to placate the Emperor by amending the law of conspiracy ; but this was regarded as shameful truckling to a foreign Power. The next important episode was the Italian crisis. Then came the American Civil War (1861-5), which not only caused a cotton famine, a grave matter for Lancashire, but bitterly divided Englishmen generally. The Polish rising of 1863 stirred both their sympathy with nationalism and their hatred of Russia. And in 1864 the Government only barely survived its abandonment of the popular Danish cause in ' the Schleswig-Holstein Question '.

To resume the quotation from G. M. Young :

Domestic politics are languid. Once, if not twice, in twenty years, the franchise had brought England in sight of civil war : in the 'fifties a Franchise Bill was four times introduced

Quater ipso in limine portae
substitit, atque utero sonitum quater arma dedere,

and was forgotten ; the annual motion on the ballot became an annual joke. Ireland was prostrate, Old Chartists were lecturing on Christian evidences, or, more usefully, working quietly in the new trade unions ; old republicans were shouting for war ; old pacifists declaiming to empty halls. Nothing is so bloody-minded as a Radical turned patriot. Roebuck was all for bombarding Naples. Bentham's former secretary, Bowring, crowned his astonishingly various career by actually bombarding Canton. Only those whose memories went back fifteen years could understand the change of sentiment which made the arming of the volunteers in '59 possible, or how completely the confidence which inspired that gesture was vindicated by the patience of Lancashire in the cotton famine.

The repeal of the Corn Laws in 1846 seemed to have satisfied middle-class reformers ; the failure of Chartism had tamed working-class agitators. Richard Cobden and John Bright, the leaders of the great Repeal movement in the 'forties, found the temper of the 'fifties and early 'sixties wholly unsympathetic.

How do you admire [asked Cobden in 1863] the reception given to [Palmerston] in Scotland ? For the Town Councils and their addresses I can find excuses. . . . But there is no doubt that the demonstration was largely shared by the working class, which is certainly one of the most singular and inexplicable of public incidents. . . .

I observe what you say about Bright's powers of eloquence. That eloquence has been most unsparingly used since the repeal of the Corn Laws—now going on for nearly twenty years—in advocating financial economy and parliamentary reform, and in every possible way for the abatement of privilege and the elevation of the masses. If he could talk till doomsday he would never surpass the strains of eloquence with which he has expounded the right and demolished the wrong cause. Yet see with what absolute lack of success ! [1]

[1] 5 April, to Mr W. Hargreaves : J. Morley, *The Life of Richard Cobden* (London, 1903, 1-vol. ed.), pp. 880-1

Of course Cobden was exaggerating. Reform had not ceased altogether. Although no great measures to match the First Reform Act or the Poor Law Amendment Act were passed during this period, Gladstone's Budgets reduced indirect taxes to a minimum, administrative reform continued steadily, and it was found possible to transform the old Universities. If the violence of Chartists and Anti-Corn Law Leaguers did not recur, agitation was carried on in milder ways. The middle class had its Administrative Reform Associations and its National Association for the Promotion of Social Science; the activity of the working class was directed at procuring small but solid economic improvements instead of vast political changes of uncertain import. But, by comparison with the Age of Grey and Peel and the Age of Gladstone and Disraeli, the Age of Palmerston was certainly 'anti-reforming times'.[1]

Cobden completed his picture in 1864, referring to Garibaldi's visit to London :

> When will the masses of this country begin to think of home politics ? Our friend Bright observed, as he gazed from a window in Parliament Street on the tens of thousands that cheered the Italian, ' If the people would only make a few such demonstrations for themselves, we could do something for them.' But nothing except foreign politics seems to occupy the attention of the people, press, or parliament.[2]

Discounting his exaggeration again, it is still clear enough that external topics were often arousing more interest than internal issues. In fact foreign affairs were furnishing a large part of the matter of domestic politics. A Government was forced to appeal to the country in 1857, and to resign in 1858, over

[1] 27 November 1860, Gladstone to Graham : C. S. Parker, *The Life and Letters of Sir James Graham* (London, 1907), vol. ii, p. 403
[2] 10 May, to Mr T. B. Potter (Morley, *Cobden*, p. 911n)

foreign questions ; and cognate disputes were important contributory causes of the changes of Administration in February 1852, 1855 and perhaps 1859. It was not until 1866 that more normal times returned and the Austro-Prussian War was ignored in the excitement of a battle over Parliamentary Reform.

Perhaps it is legitimate to carry the argument even further. What seem at first sight to be the domestic issues of the period often had an external bearing. 'Papal Aggression'—the reestablishment of the Roman Catholic hierarchy in England—which aroused indignation in 1850, is an obvious example. The demand for Administrative Reform grew during the Crimean War. Cobden and Bright turned after the Repeal of the Corn Laws to advocating not only the extension of Free Trade by commercial treaties but also what they regarded as its logical corollary, the general reduction of armaments. And the cause of Parliamentary Reform profited by its association with enthusiasm for freedom in Italy, Poland and the Northern States of America. It would appear that domestic issues could flourish only in connexion with some external interest. This is a most exceptional period. While it is true that in eighteenth-century politics Hanover was a crucial issue ; that nothing so decisive in its effect on English affairs as the French Revolution disturbed the mid-Victorians ; and that in the early and late nineteenth century the English on occasion showed great interest in external matters, as during the Greek War of Independence, at the time of the Midlothian Campaign or in the Imperialist years : there is no parallel to the overriding public concern with foreign questions which distinguished the Age of Palmerston.

It is characteristic of the years between 1846 and 1868—a period nearly conterminous with the Age of Palmerston—that Governments are weak, parties disorganised and public opinion powerful. Of the seven Ministries which held office during this time, four at least had only minority support in the House of Commons, and none had a large and reliable majority. This is the one period of any length when the House has been able to exercise freely what Walter Bagehot called in his classic work, *The English Constitution*, published in 1867, ' the elective function ' of choosing a Cabinet.[1] Before the First Reform Act of 1832 the monarch could usually reckon that Ministers of his preference would secure a majority in the Commons and in the country. After the Second Reform Act of 1867 the electorate generally determined the issue between rival Front Benches. In the interval, and especially after 1846, Members could often make the choice for themselves. This is the moment of equilibrium : royal and Government patronage has dwindled so far that it can exert little influence ; the franchise has yet to be widely extended, and so the voters have yet to be disciplined by centralised parties ; and many individual Members, owing their seats to private patronage or local reputation, can afford to be independent of party. In the General Election of 1857, it is true, the electorate reversed Parliament's verdict against Palmerston's Government. But otherwise the House of Commons was supreme from 1846 until 1868. On four occasions, in February 1852, 1855, 1858 and 1866, it displaced the strongest available Administration and then for a while tolerated a weaker successor. Ministers had only one resource, dissolution ; and that was an unsatisfactory weapon, since, as with the bee's sting, to use it was commonly fatal to the user. There were four dissolutions between 1850 and 1867 ; each time, although the Government gained a few seats, it was turned out within a year. Members were freest just after one General Election, because no-one wanted another to follow quickly. Strictly speaking, the

[1] World's Classics edition (Oxford, 1928), p. 117

Commons did not 'elect' Ministries, as Bagehot said they did ; they could only reject them. It was the Queen and senior statesmen who had to find new combinations acceptable to the House. The task was often very difficult ; and it once proved actually impossible, in 1851, when Russell's Government, having resigned, had to be ignominiously reinstated. The executive has never been more in the power of the House than during this period.

Parliamentary parties had been remarkably coherent in the Age of Grey and Peel ; and for much of the decade 1835–45 almost every M.P. had been classifiable as either Liberal or Conservative. The Conservative split over the Corn Laws in 1845 transformed the political situation. During the Age of Palmerston there were usually more than two parties in the House ; and party discipline was decidedly weaker than in the earlier period. The name 'Conservative' came to be monopolised by those who had opposed Peel's Free Trade policy, while those who had supported it acted as a third party, originally numbering over a hundred and including most of his ablest Cabinet colleagues, known as 'the Peelites'. The rank-and-file Peelites soon made their peace with the Conservative party ; most of the chiefs, on the other hand, joined with the Liberals in the Coalition Government of Lord Aberdeen, then broke away from Palmerston, and were out of office until 1859, when they were at last effectively absorbed into the Liberal party. Not only was Peel's old following divided ; so, after 1850, were the Liberals. The Liberal party had been a virtual coalition between various types of Whig, Liberal and Radical, together with the Irish Roman Catholic M.P.s. In the 'fifties this complex was broken up : an independent Irish party was created ; and the leadership of the Liberals was disputed between Palmerston and Russell. The formation of Palmerston's second Ministry reunited the party.

But after his death it split again, over Parliamentary Reform. Plainly these divisions helped greatly to undermine party discipline. But this is not the whole story. For, even when the two-party system was temporarily re-established after 1859, political allegiances were less binding on members than they had been before 1846 or would be from 1868 onwards.[1]

According to Napoleon III and Cavour at Plombières, the English Government was the slave of public opinion. Particularly between 1853 and 1858 politicians found themselves at the mercy of popular movements in the country. First the Aberdeen Government was forced into the Crimean War. Next in 1855 the House of Commons as the agent of opinion brought down the same Government, and drove the Peelites and Russell from office. At the General Election of 1857 the Commons' verdict against Palmerston's Ministry was reversed. Then in 1858 Palmerston himself, the beneficiary of these earlier movements, suffered for his sympathy with France. While the memory of these experiences was still fresh in their minds, statesmen were inclined to pay, if anything, too much respect to public opinion. Of course, in the normal way, it was only through the House of Commons that the public could actually enforce respect for its views. But the House was believed to represent opinion with remarkable accuracy. This was the *Saturday Review*'s comment on the ministerial crisis of 1858 :

The fall of Lord Palmerston's Administration, and the apparently final collapse of his popularity in the early part of the session, are events which the students of political history will do well attentively to consider. The first conclusion which they will be disposed to draw will certainly not be that to which the unscrupulous demagogues of the platform seem so anxious to bring us—viz.

[1] There are some incomplete but suggestive statistics in A. L. Lowell, *The Government of England* (London, 1912), vol. ii, pp. 76n and 79n.

that the present constitution of the House of Commons is a
fraudulent contrivance for evading the representation of public
opinion. No sooner was it really felt that popular feeling had
decidedly pronounced against Lord Palmerston's Government,
than it fell helplessly and hopelessly in a Parliament which had
been elected not twelve months before amidst shouts of ' Palmerston
for ever '. Partisan critics may blame, if they please, the mutability
of public opinion, but to charge the House of Commons with want
of sympathy with the popular voice is either to expose their
ignorance or confess their prejudice.[1]

The looseness of party discipline in the Commons enabled
Members to respond with alacrity to outside influences ;
Governments avoided more frequent Parliamentary censure
only by responding more quickly still. Without Bismarck's
army, English Ministers could not afford Bismarck's ' realism '.
They did not profess to be able fully to understand the pheno-
menon of public opinion ; they thought there must inevitably
be an element of mystery about it. But they hoped they could
recognise it. Bagehot laid famous emphasis on the ' deference '
of the English nation. Equally significant was the deference of
its rulers.

Sidney Herbert, one of Peel's old Cabinet colleagues,
attempted a survey of the general political situation in the
no-confidence debate of 1859 :

I do not think we shall get from it what may be called a strong
Government ; many lament that ; they say parties are broken up,
and that is lamented also, without recognizing the causes. Though
some political questions may bring masses in the House together,
yet the tendency on both sides is to break up the old lines of party.
You will never get a strong Government in that sense ; nor do I
think we want a strong Government in the sense the country did
formerly. Then society was weak, and a strong Government was

[1] 1 January 1859

necessary to repress and guide it, now society is strong and domi-
nates the Government set over it.[1]

It may be suggested that the public's concern with external
topics was a contributory factor here. As long as foreign
questions engross attention, stable party alignments are unlikely
to be formed. Most international crises are short-lived, and
so are the issues they raise ; moreover, when the country's
vital interests are obviously at stake, the instinct of self-
preservation tends to produce a common sentiment. It is
only very rarely that divisions over foreign policy are fundamental and enduring, as they were during the French Revolutionary and Napoleonic Wars. The party system thrives best
on broad, deep and lasting disagreements over social policy.

II

The exceptional interest in foreign affairs which had been
kindled by the 1848 Revolutions and the subsequent Reaction
was associated with the dominance of a particular national
mood which the same crisis had evoked. Till then, France
had been Liberal ; there had even appeared, it was thought,
a Liberal Pope. The victory of absolutism on the Continent,
seen most strikingly in the usurpation of Napoleon III, left
Englishmen the only notable defenders of civil liberty surviving
in Europe ; the Catholic Reaction, signalised to England by
'Papal Aggression', and apparently closely linked with the
absolutists' triumph, threatened religious liberty. Protestantism and Liberalism, the double heritage of the 1688 Revolution,
seemed to be in equal peril. The English now became much
more self-conscious and active propagandists of their ideology.
Their complacency about internal affairs was enhanced by their

[1] *Parl. Deb.*, 3rd series, vol. cliv, col. 334 (10 June 1859)

conviction that they could no longer be complacent about the external situation. The country must be strong enough to resist any invading despot, and it must be prepared to sustain constitutionalism in Europe, perhaps even by force. When in 1847 the Duke of Wellington had expressed alarm at the strength of France and the weakness of England, only the Government had shown interest ; in 1852 the Government was compelled by popular clamour and Palmerston to embody 80,000 militiamen. Though a year later Russia succeeded France as the principal bogy, the same mood remained dominant. The Crimean War was advocated as a War of Liberation ; and Martin Tupper, uncritical in this as in other ways of the banalities of his age, wrote to his friend Gladstone in 1855 : ' I side with those who are *at war* with *Russia* and *Rome*, with earthly and spiritual despotisms ; and who stand for the liberty of enslaved nations and consciences.' [1] In the Orsini crisis the prejudice against France reappeared—despite the fact that she had been England's ally in the Crimean War —in company with the same over-sensitive nationalism and readiness to defy a despot. There was another invasion panic in 1859 and 1860. And the rights of British citizens abroad were jealously guarded.

Of course this mood was not fully shared by all Englishmen. Most statesmen opposed Palmerston in the Don Pacifico debate and over the China War ; Palmerston himself, where Napoleon III was concerned, did not please those who condemned all truckling to foreign Powers ; and Cobden and Bright were chiefly concerned with the peaceful propagation of Free Trade doctrine. But the history of the 'fifties shows clearly that the dominant mood was that described above.

In the context of this general outlook it was natural that Englishmen should sympathise with any national movement

[1] 26 November : D. Hudson, *Martin Tupper* (London, 1949), p. 210

on the part of constitutionalists against a despotic Power. The Italian movement was no exception. In fact it was on several counts uniquely attractive to Englishmen, and the nature of the attraction was such that they developed—long before 1859—a definite and in some respects a distinctive attitude to the Italian Question.

Well-educated Englishmen thinking of Italy conjured up before anything else the image of Imperial Rome. Their classical training induced a special interest in Italy, and might lead them to wonder whether the political acumen of the ancient Romans could have deserted the inhabitants of the peninsula so completely that they were now incapable of governing themselves well, or even at all. The civilisation of Italy in the late Middle Ages and Renaissance was also much admired and studied. Throughout the nineteenth century Italian inspiration was of major importance in the visual arts, though taste veered from post-Raphaelite to pre-Raphaelite, and Palladian gave way to Venetian Gothic. To the early Romantics especially, Italian literature had been most attractive : Italian had for a while become, after French, the fashionable language ; and Dante had enjoyed a great vogue. Some of this enthusiasm lasted into the 'fifties and beyond. In every aspect of cultural activity the Italians were recognised to have been at some time pre-eminent. And grand opera continued to be almost exclusively Italian until after 1860. Englishmen were therefore inclined to doubt, with Gladstone :

whether anywhere in Christendom there be an instance corresponding with the Austrian power in Italy ; an instance where a people glaringly inferior in refinement rule, and that by the medium of arbitrary will, without the check of free institutions, over a race much more advanced.[1]

[1] W. E. Gladstone, 'War in Italy', *Quarterly Review*, vol. cv (1859), pp. 549–50

Too much must not be made of English interest in Italian culture proper. Compelling as that interest was to the generation that was young between 1815 and 1840, it seems to have been a wasting asset in the middle years of the nineteenth century. By the 'fifties Germany had come into her own in literature, philosophy and instrumental music. The appeal of classical culture, however, did not diminish. This fact, together with the beauty of the country, ensured that Italy remained the most favoured destination of English travellers. As Dr G. M. Trevelyan says :

> If foreign travel was less common than to-day, it was more concentrated upon Italy ; and the charm of her landscapes and cities became associated in sympathetic English minds with the cause of the inhabitants of the country. Indeed, it was impossible to visit the peninsula without seeing clear signs of an odious oppression.[1]

The large colony of English artists and writers resident in Italy, particularly in Florence, included many strong supporters of Italian Liberalism, and their writings of course influenced readers at home. These various contacts were most important in arousing interest in Italy ; and they served on the whole to strengthen Englishmen's sympathy with the Italian cause.[2]

Equally significant in arousing English interest in the Italian Question, and far more significant in giving Englishmen a distinctive attitude towards it, was Protestantism. The ordinary Englishman thinking of Italy remembered first the Pope of Rome ; and even for those who thought first of the Empire the image of the Scarlet Woman was more vivid.

[1] G. M. Trevelyan, ' Englishmen and Italians ', in *Clio, A Muse, and Other Essays* (London, 1930), p. 114

[2] I am principally indebted for the material of these two paragraphs to Dr Trevelyan's lecture cited in the previous note, to C. P. Brand, *Italy and the English Romantics* (Cambridge, 1957), and to G. Artom Treves, *The Golden Ring* (London, 1956).

My use of the term ' Renaissance ' is not intended to imply that the men of 1859 would have used it in the same sense. On this point see J. R. Hale, *England and the Italian Renaissance* (London, 1954).

Ancient history aroused genteel interest and prompted scholarly reflection ; modern Papalism provoked popular indignation. Roman Catholicism was hateful to the mass of Englishmen as the arch-enemy of all liberty ; it was still a political as well as a religious bugbear. Any opponent of the Papacy was the ally of England. Most Englishmen would believe, and wished to hear, any enormity credited to Roman Catholicism. It was always easy to make a stir with a report of some new iniquity in Rome : in 1858 and the following year the abduction of a Jew, Mortara, was much canvassed. Few Don Juans have achieved the success that Protestant legend ascribed to confessors.[1] Apostate Roman Catholic priests, like Gavazzi and Achilli, were certain of an audience in England. The irritation caused by the Oxford Movement, regarded as the thin end of the Papal wedge, strengthened the opposition of Evangelicals and Nonconformists to Romanism. The Anglo-Catholic view, as held by Gladstone, that a reformed Papacy 'doing well' would be a matter for joy, was extremely rare. Much more congenial were his denunciations of the existing condition, 'a foul blot upon the face of creation, an offence to Christendom and to mankind'.[2] This religious interest was far more widespread than the literary and artistic interest, far more fervent and far more closely related to the political question. The English readily sympathised with Italians who saw the Temporal Power barring their way to freedom. It was easy to forget that Liberal Italians were in fact generally good Roman Catholics.

[1] For example, there is in the Archivio del Ministero degli Affari Esteri in Rome (correspondence of the Sardinian Legation in London, Cartella lxxxix : see Ministero degli Affari Esteri, *Indici dell' Archivio Storico* (Rome, 1947–), vol. iv, for classification) a Protestant pamphlet recounting the sad fate of 33 'young females' 'ruined' by one priest in the Confessional. One T. P. Monaghan had written to ask if it was true (25 August 1860).

[2] W. E. Gladstone, 'Farini's *Stato Romano*', *Edinburgh Review*, vol. xcv (1852), p. 382

Piedmont's anti-clerical legislation and the Liberals' desire to secularise Italian government naturally endeared them to the English. When Cavour visited London in 1856, he found that 'the most enthusiastic [for the Italian cause] are the Protestant zealots headed by Lord Shaftesbury. If they were listened to, England would start a crusade against Austria.'[1] They were the most consistent supporters of the struggle for Italian freedom, understanding by that phrase more particularly religious freedom. In consequence, they were also the keenest admirers of Piedmont, as the one Italian state to accord this boon to its subjects : the fate of its 'Waldensians', the descendants of medieval heretics, had for centuries been a concern of English Protestantism. A wider circulation of Bibles was expected to follow the expulsion of Austria. Some even hoped for the conversion of Italy as a whole. King Victor Emanuel and Garibaldi were felt to be equally deserving of recognition for their opposition to Papal claims, and both were presented with numerous Protestant addresses, and even Bibles.[2] Cavour and any other Italian anti-Papalists, however sincerely Roman Catholic, had here a large body of ready-made support, which the Piedmontese were careful to cultivate. Emanuele d'Azeglio, their envoy in London, writing to Cavour in May 1859, mentioned that a Biblical society was anxious to congratulate the Florentines on attaining religious liberty and that he had promised one of their agents a letter of introduction : 'Pray welcome him', he said, 'and arrange for him to be served plenty of holy water, for this party can be most useful to us at this time.'[3] Garibaldi, too, was amenable to Protestant influence. In 1860 he gave

[1] 20 April, to Rattazzi (*CC Ing.*, vol. ii, part i, p. 1)
[2] On Victor Emanuel C. C. F. Greville, *A Journal of the Reign of Queen Victoria from 1852 to 1860* (London, 1887), vol. i [i.e. *The Greville Memoirs*, vol. vii], p. 303 ; and on Garibaldi esp. G. Sacerdote, *La Vita di Giuseppe Garibaldi* (Milan, 1933), p. 589   [3] *CC Ing.*, vol. ii, part i, p. 331

land in Naples for a Protestant church ; and he was ready to commend church bazaars.[1] The active good offices of Lord Shaftesbury, not only effective head of the Evangelicals, but also son-in-law of Palmerston, were always available to respectable Italian patriots. Austria, on the other hand, had concluded a Concordat with the Papacy in 1855, thus further alienating English sympathy. Protestant feeling, both among the more ardent and among the mass of Englishmen, was firmly pro-Italian and, especially, pro-Piedmontese. Gladstone's claim that Englishmen demonstrated their religious impartiality by favouring the efforts of Roman Catholics in Italy is distinctly optimistic ; rather, Protestants in a confused way believed Cavour's to be a Protestant programme.[2]

It has often been charged that English support for Italian freedom sprang from selfish economic motives, from interest in the sulphur mines of Sicily, hope of railway promotion, or happy anticipation of more markets for English produce in a tariff-free Italy.[3] There are examples of direct connexions between commerce and politics : Joseph Cowen, one of Mazzini's closest friends, traded with Italy. It cannot be denied that Cavour's fiscal successes—or apparent fiscal successes—made Piedmont a safer area of investment for English bankers and businessmen, nor that the impression of financial stability he created made a favourable impact in England. He had negotiated with English firms for railway contracts.[4] He certainly had in mind when lowering Piedmontese import duties the pleasure this would give in England, and no doubt

---

[1] O. W. S. Chambers, *Garibaldi and Italian Unity* (London, 1864), pp. 114 and 270n

[2] Gladstone's statement was in a speech at Manchester (*The Times*, 15 October 1864). See, in general, G. Spini, *Risorgimento e Protestanti* (Naples, 1956).

[3] e.g., A. Zazo, *La Politica Estera del Regno delle Due Sicilie nel 1859–60* (Naples, 1940), *passim*, esp. p. 322n

[4] See F. Arese, *Cavour e le Strade Ferrate* (Milan, 1953)

he improved thereby the prospects of English products. But it is not possible to link particular economic calculations with the widespread pro-Italian feeling in England. It can even be shown that in certain cases English commerce actually suffered by the extension to the rest of Italy of the Piedmontese tariff, as with the formerly free port of Leghorn.[1] Faith in the overall blessings of Free Trade, on the other hand, was a principal tenet of the Liberal religion of the mid-nineteenth century. It was, of course, of universal application, and did not relate to Italy more than, say, to Prussia. But by ostentatiously espousing it Cavour undoubtedly increased the popularity of Piedmont in England.

Apart from these general grounds of interest, literary and artistic, religious and economic, there were two special factors enhancing the strength and affecting the nature of English pro-Italian feeling. The first, the vital importance of which did not become apparent until 1860, was hero-worship of Garibaldi. The second, of deep significance in 1860 but also effective earlier, was detestation of the King of Naples.

Unlike Kossuth, who in any case never attained quite the same level of fame, Garibaldi was well known even before his greatest exploits. His achievements as a guerrilla leader in South America and Rome had been publicised by the *Illustrated London News* in the 'fifties and had made him already one of the most celebrated of world-figures in England. *Punch* later pointed out, through the mouth of a ' snob ', that he was ' a revolootionary leader, similar to those in the penypapers '.[2] When he had visited Tyneside in 1854 he had been accorded an enthusiastic reception by the working men of Blaydon.[3] His notoriety ensured that his part in the

---

[1] N. Blakiston, 'L'Inghilterra e la Tariffa Piemontese, 1859–60', *Rassegna storica del Risorgimento*, vol. xliv (1957), pp. 312–14   [2] 23 April 1864
[3] G. M. Trevelyan, *Garibaldi and the Thousand* (London, 1909), p. 25

Franco-Austrian War received exceptional and unusually favourable publicity. The great advantage which his reputation brought to the Italian cause was the extension of its appeal to the English working class without loss of its attraction to the more sophisticated. He was the ideal champion of the cause—romantic, heroic, simple and disinterested.

Gladstone, then a Conservative in home politics and one of Palmerston's accusers in the Don Pacifico debate, visited Naples in 1850. What he saw there—the mockery of a trial of some Liberals and the ghastly conditions of their subsequent imprisonment—so stirred him that he published in July 1851, under the title *Two Letters to Lord Aberdeen*, an indictment of the Neapolitan state before public opinion.[1] His condemnation was summed up in the phrase he quoted from the lips of some subject of the King of the Two Sicilies, who described its administration as 'the negation of God erected into a system of government'. Contrary to his previous position, Gladstone now recognised that some of the old régimes were decadent beyond recall, and came to think that the case of Naples was so intolerable as to justify 'forcible intervention by the authority of Europe or of such a combination of Powers as may claim to represent it for the purpose'.[2] Englishmen already had an unpleasant picture of King Ferdinand II, 'Bomba', who had in 1849 bombarded his own cities and broken his oath to the constitution. Now this impression was strengthened, and in fact from this time virtually no-one in England can be found to say a good word for the Neapolitan state. Almost any attack on it would be condoned.

Englishmen, then, were in no doubt that the governments of Rome and Naples were in need of drastic reform, perhaps

---

[1] W. E. Gladstone, *Two Letters to the Earl of Aberdeen, on the State Prosecutions of the Neapolitan Government* (London, 1851)
[2] 25 October 1856, to Lacaita (GP BM Add MS 44233, f.63)

past reform. They disliked the idea of Austrian dominance over Italy. Piedmont, because of her Liberal religious and economic policy, was the particular object of their goodwill towards Italy. And in time they would cheerfully support Garibaldi against ' Bomba '.

Yet fundamentally, despite these exceptional grounds of interest and these specific opinions on certain points, the attitude of the English to Italy's plight was their usual attitude to the troubles of other countries. Their recipe for the cure of all the world's political ills, and a good part of any other ills, was constitutional government. Their principal reason for admiring Piedmont was her adhesion to the constitutional camp in Europe. As the Prince Consort pointed out to his brother :

> Ever since 1817 the British people have been striving for liberty and self-determination at home, and for the same in Europe. During the same period Austria headed the attacks on the liberty and independence of peoples. . . . There is no need to explain how it came about that Sardinia, in her character of the only tolerant and constitutional State in Italy in spite of her perilous situation between Austria, France, and the Pope, holds England's fullest sympathies.[1]

In the rest of Italy it was assumed that the proper solution would be the introduction of constitutional reforms in the existing states. The English greatly underestimated the difficulties in the way. They thought that, if Naples only had a King who would enforce the constitution of 1848, if the Pope would merely put into effect the measures promised by the *Motu proprio* of 1849, if even Austria would administer Lombardy and Venetia better and separately from her other possessions, and if she would only leave the Italian states to

---

[1] 18 June 1859, Prince Albert to Duke Ernest II of Saxe-Coburg-Gotha : ed. K. Jagow, *Letters of the Prince Consort* (London, 1938), pp. 337–8

themselves so that Liberal Reform could peacefully prevail—
then Italy would be free and happy. They reasoned from the
myths of their own history. 1688 had opened a new era for
England. The same sort of bloodless revolution could do as
much for the Italians. Very few Englishmen considered in
making up their prescriptions how exceptional was the case-
history of their own country. The insular security, the overwhelming wealth and the extraordinary advantages which
had enabled England to reach her present blessed condition
were discounted. The difficulties which had been overcome,
and those still remaining, were forgotten. It was assumed
that a little effort would make constitutional government
work in any civilised state. As for Piedmont's attitude to
the troubles of the rest of the peninsula, she must be patient.
Gladstone put the point typically :

> It may be in the designs of Providence that she shall one day be
> territorially great : but if she is to attain to that kind of greatness
> and to join with it any durability of power, it must be by the
> slow growth of the oak, by the prolonged exercise of self-command
> and self-denial, by the careful development of her industry and
> her internal resources, by disinterested service to her sister States
> in Italy, and above all by the strictest respect for every political
> and legal right.[1]

This was the respectable English view, held with varying
intensity but almost universal. Piedmont was favoured as a
peaceful, progressive, Liberal, constitutional example to Italy.
It was envisaged that she would act as a bastion not only
against Austria and the Pope, but also against other despotic
Powers, more especially France and Russia. By adopting
another role she would forfeit English sympathy. Cavour
could hardly feel satisfied with the English attitude to the
Italian Question.

[1] Gladstone, Q.R., vol. cv (1859), p. 552

Still less could Mazzini. During twenty years of exile in England he had been combating these insular prejudices in the hope of imposing his own view, that Italy would rise and unite herself if only given the opportunity. His influence in England has often been rated high. He made many English friends and became widely respected ; he conducted a vigorous propaganda campaign ; he joined in and helped to plan the work of English societies which sympathised with nationalism ; and he was able to collect, over a long period, a considerable sum of money. The outcry raised against the Home Office on his behalf when it tampered with his correspondence in 1844, and his striking achievements as triumvir of the Roman Republic in 1849, made him a public figure in England. Blaydon's address of welcome to Garibaldi in 1854 even spoke of the great hero as a mere coadjutor of Mazzini.[1] But Tyneside in 1854 was a very special case. In the words of Mazzini's biographer, Bolton King :

> As far as money went, Mazzini got less than he hoped from his English agitation. A few friends gave generously, but there was little of the response that came to Garibaldi's appeal a few years later. But the Society [of the Friends of Italy] did much to win English opinion, if not for Mazzini's own special schemes, at all events for the bigger question of Italian liberty.[2]

That is the crux of the matter. Even some of Mazzini's closest associates regarded his fully-developed schemes for the unification of Italy by revolution as visionary, and were reluctant to back him wholeheartedly : his letters are full of complaints at the slowness and smallness of his friend Peter Taylor's subscriptions ; even Cowen, to judge from his newspapers, the *Newcastle Chronicle* and the *Newcastle Daily Chronicle*, did not hold

[1] The address was on show at the 1954 exhibition at the Italian Institute in London, ' Garibaldi's Visit to Newcastle in 1854 '.
[2] Bolton King, *The Life of Mazzini* (London, 1912), p. 153

to the full doctrine of the prophet. Implicit acceptance of his personal beliefs, rare in any case, was usually short-lived. Many of the members of the moderate pro-Italian party in England, as with the Liberals in Italy, were half committed to his creed for a time early in their careers ; but very few people, and those mostly women, remained disciples for long. He was reduced to employing the small change of English Protestant and Radical arguments : invoking Italy's services to civilisation ; praising ' liberty of conscience, which can only be proclaimed for the whole of Europe by the overthrow of the Papacy at Rome ' ; urging the danger of ' secrecy in international communications ' and the need ' to found your own international life—to declare your sympathy—to pave the way by acts for the New Alliances, which will replace in the future your own Britain on that honourable basis of policy which has been forsaken since the days of Cromwell '.[1] Mazzini undoubtedly aroused and sustained interest, but it was not always interest even in Italian liberty, let alone in his own schemes. He has been so much idolised that it seems worth pointing out that he sometimes repelled people.[2] His advocacy of the Italian cause did much to compromise its respectability. Unlike Garibaldi, he won virtually no support among the upper classes, while his appeal to the working class was too intellectual and esoteric to be widely effective. ' Red Revolution ' alarmed many more Englishmen than it attracted. And increasingly through the 'fifties it became obvious that Mazzini's revolutions were working against the fulfilment of reasonable Italian hopes. Apart from the wastage in lives

[1] 2 March 1857, to the Secretary of the Committee for aiding the Emancipation of Italy : *Scritti editi ed inediti di Giuseppe Mazzini* (Imola, 1906–), vol. lxvii, pp. 337–8
[2] cf. Gladstone's view : J. Morley, *The Life of William Ewart Gladstone* (London, 1903), vol. i, p. 402 and vol. iii, p. 478. Or the Duke of Somerset's : ed. W. H. Mallock and Lady G. Ramsden, *Letters, etc. of . . . Somerset* (London, 1893), p. 313

and the futility of his expectation that the whole peninsula would rise, the Genoa insurrection of 1857 finally made it clear that his plots were hampering, and were designed to hamper, the progress of Liberal Piedmont. Mazzini by 1859 was a lone figure in England. It is not certain whether his activity had on the whole benefited the Italian cause there ; and it is plain that, on the ordinary English attitude to the Italian Question, the influence of his ideology was negligible.[1]

There was no lack of notable figures besides Mazzini among the numerous Italian exiles in England, both Mazzinians and Cavourians. Of Mazzinians, Orsini made the greatest impact : he was a popular speaker and, after his attempt on the life of Napoleon III, something of a hero to many Englishmen. His plot and its sequel served to underline the differences which inevitably separated the Emperor from Italian patriots, differences which Englishmen continued to exaggerate in relation to Cavour as well as to the revolutionaries. Of Cavourians, Antonio Panizzi, Principal Librarian of the British Museum, a Modenese by origin, was easily the foremost. He made little effort to influence public opinion on a large scale ; but his extensive Italian correspondence and his loyalty to Cavour, coupled with his friendship with Gladstone, Palmerston and Russell, enabled him to serve the moderate Piedmontese party very effectively. He played a large part in the preparation of the *Letters to Lord Aberdeen*, and he was to be used on several occasions as an intermediary by both Cavour and Russell.[2] Giacomo Lacaita, a Neapolitan, though a less staunch supporter of Cavour and of the Italian cause in general, was nevertheless

[1] For a full and more sympathetic account of Mazzinian and Radical activity see D. F. Mackay, 'The Influence of the Italian Risorgimento on British " Public Opinion " . . .' (unpublished D.Phil. thesis, Oxford University, 1959).

[2] C. Brooks, *Antonio Panizzi* (Manchester, 1931), esp. chs. v and vi

valuable to Piedmont as another friend of the pro-Italian ministerial triumvirate and another possible go-between.[1] But the influence of the exiles as a whole, like that of Mazzini, was equivocal : their presence in England was a perpetual reminder of the lack of liberty in Italy ; but their activities were often distasteful even to their well-wishers. And throughout the period there was friction between the two groups of Mazzinians and Cavourians. The Neapolitan exiles of 1859 soon divided themselves into two sections on the same lines, making the task of the reception committee very delicate.[2] The difficulty arose again with Garibaldi's visit of 1864, when there was competition to entertain him. Such evidence of Italian disunity did not encourage English support. Moreover, since the same division recurred among enthusiastic English pro-Italians, the more extreme views of both parties tended to cancel each other out.

Surprisingly few Englishmen, however, were actually committed to either group. Just as virtually no-one accepted all Mazzini's teaching, so there was scarcely a strict English Cavourian : even some of the most favourable, like Shaftesbury and Gladstone, had considerable reservations. Perhaps the nearest case was that of Sir James Hudson, the English Minister to Turin, whom Cavour described as more ' Italian ' than himself.[3] Undoubtedly the normal English attitude, if neither Mazzinian nor Cavourian, was ' pro-Italian ' in a sense. And there was this degree of justice in the claim of the English that only they viewed the Italian problem without partisan bias and with an eye to the different needs of the various parts

[1] C. Lacaita, *An Italian Englishman* (London, 1933), esp. ch. vi
[2] *CC Ing.*, vol. ii, part i, pp. 258–86. Paolo Romano (P. Alatri), *Silvio Spaventa* (Bari, 1942), pp. 89–93
[3] *The Greville Memoirs*, vol. viii, p. 282. See the Introduction to Hudson's diplomatic correspondence : ed. F. Curato, *Le Relazioni Diplomatiche tra la Gran Bretagna ed il Regno di Sardegna dal 1852 al 1856* (Turin, 1956), vol. i, pp. xi–xxvii

of Italy : the average English sympathiser with Italian aspirations was quite innocent of any notion of ' Piedmontisation '
or enforced Italian unity ; he genuinely wished to see Italians
politically free, and he would subordinate this wish to no
other consideration. But this broad outlook was not combined
with an understanding of the political realities, which Cavour
so well appreciated, nor with a recognition of the potential
strength of national feeling, which Mazzini in his eccentric
way had grasped. The English, like the early Italian Liberals,
failed to realise how obdurate Austria was and therefore how
necessary her expulsion from Italy would be ; and so they
did not see that the Italian Question was inevitably an international problem, and also a problem for the whole peninsula.
They regarded it as a matter of ' local freedom and reform
in the several states '.[1]

III

England's official policy had often reflected this attitude.
In 1847—to go no further back—Lord Minto, a Cabinet
Minister, had been sent to urge reforms in all the states of
the peninsula. In 1848, when there seemed to be hope of
Piedmontese expansion in North Italy, the English Government was delighted ; it was divided only on the question
whether, while Austria was weak, to settle for the cession
of Lombardy to Piedmont, or to demand Venetia in addition.
During the Crimean War England welcomed Piedmont's
alliance against Russia. Lord Clarendon, the Foreign Secretary, took advantage of the Congress of Paris to attack in
strong terms Austria's Italian policy. And shortly afterwards
the English Government joined with the French in withdraw-

[1] W. E. Gladstone, *Gleanings of Past Years* (London, 1879), vol. iv,
p. 195n

ing its diplomatic representatives from Naples in protest against the misrule of her King.

These were the acts of Liberal Governments. The Italian sympathies of the Conservatives were thought to be tepid. But the Conservative Ministry of Lord Derby, formed in 1858 with Lord Malmesbury as Foreign Secretary, took the part of Piedmont in the affair of the steamer *Cagliari*, a Piedmontese vessel seized by the Neapolitans because it had lately been used by Mazzinian revolutionaries. In fact, other things being equal, all English statesmen wished to assist the progress of Liberalism abroad ; and even the Queen thought :

It must ever be our object and interest to see Sardinia independent and strong ; as a Liberal constitutional country, opposing a barrier alike to unenlightened and absolute as well as revolutionary principles—and this she has a right to expect us to support her in.[1]

[1] 9 January 1856, to Clarendon (*QVL*, vol. iii, p. 161)

Chapter III

The Approach to War

1 January to 19 April 1859 [1]

AT his customary New Year's Day reception to the Diplomatic Corps, the French Emperor remarked to the Austrian Ambassador : ' I regret that our relations are not as good as I would wish them to be.' [2] Whether he so intended or no, he thereby confirmed the suspicions aroused by the Plombières meeting. Even though the details of the plot remained uncertain, few experienced observers doubted any longer, taking into account the general international situation, that he was contemplating war against Austria ; and it was clear enough that such a war would be fought in Italy, with France as the ally of Piedmont, ostensibly as a war of Italian liberation. Subsequent events served only to strengthen this impression. King Victor Emanuel, in a speech on 10 January at the opening of the Piedmontese Parliament, made a provocative reference to the ' cry of pain ' from so many parts of Italy. On 30 January Prince Napoleon married Princess Clotilde. And on

---

[1] I was greatly assisted in preparing this chapter and the next, especially the sections on foreign policy, by H. Hearder, ' The Foreign Policy of Lord Malmesbury, 1858–9 ' (unpublished Ph.D. thesis, London University, 1954). Many of the relevant findings are in H. Hearder, ' La Politica di Lord Malmesbury verso l'Italia nella Primavera del 1859 ', *Rass. stor. del Ris.*, vol. xliii (1956), pp. 35–58.

[2] Comte de Hübner, *Neuf Ans de Souvenirs d'Un Ambassadeur d'Autriche à Paris* . . . (Paris, 1904), p. 244. This seems the most authentic of the many versions of this remark.

4 February an obviously 'inspired' pamphlet appeared in Paris, arguing that the Italian states ought to introduce reforms and federate themselves.[1] France and Piedmont had in fact concluded a treaty embodying most of the main provisions of the Plombières agreement—though not the federation proposal—at the end of January.[2] The Italian crisis had begun, and the Italian problem had to be faced by the Powers.

I

It was not the local constitutional problem which the English had hitherto pictured and to which their attitude was well established. An international dispute over Italy was a very different matter, and would be viewed from a very different standpoint. For the Government at least, considerations of power-politics would outweigh ideological sympathies.

Few things could be more unwelcome to official England than French intervention in Italy. It would be intervention nominally in a cause which she approved, by a Power with which she was supposed to be allied. But Napoleon's motives were suspect, and the expansion of France was dreaded. No diplomatist was able to trust French statements of policy, because the Emperor's own were disingenuous, and those of his Foreign Minister, Count Walewski, were often made in ignorance of the Emperor's secret plans. In any case, to the English, France was almost as much a culprit as Austria in the Italian Question : she had a garrison in Rome, as Austria had in the Romagna. It was hard to believe that she would not try to impose her rule, or at least to exercise an influence

[1] Entitled L'Empereur Napoléon III et l'Italie
[2] On the date of the treaty see P. Matter, Cavour et l'Unité italienne (Paris, 1927), vol. iii, p. 132, n4

as strong as Austria's had been, on any provinces she helped to conquer for Piedmont : her victory would merely change the Italians' master. England could not look forward with pleasure to the prospect of France controlling the Italian sea-board, which must threaten her own position in the Mediter-ranean. The Emperor would undoubtedly demand some territorial compensation ; and it was impossible to tell how far his ambition to emulate his uncle, the great Napoleon, might extend. Despite his frequent protestations of loyalty to the English alliance, and although his record as an ally was not unworthy, English statesmen could not rid themselves of the fear that the Italian adventure might be only the first stage in a career of conquest intended to culminate in the invasion of England.

More generally, it was to the interest of England, as a great imperial Power outside Europe and a great commercial Power within it, that peace should be preserved on the Conti-nent. If war did break out, she might prefer to remain neutral. But, especially if it spread beyond Italy, she might feel herself unable to avoid taking part. Her pre-eminence depended on the existence of a Balance of Power in Europe and therefore, it seemed, on the maintenance of the Treaties of 1815 and 1856, which secured the Continent from attempts at hegemony by the two Powers, France and Russia, most likely to bid for it. The force of the Vienna settlement would be much weakened if Napoleon succeeded in his Italian aims ; and it might be altogether overthrown if war spread. English statesmen feared that war might also lead to a revision of the Paris settlement, with Russia expanding into the Balkans at the expense of the Ottoman Empire. This, it was believed, would undermine England's position as the greatest Power in the world by threatening her overland communications with her Indian Empire. In August 1858

Russia had been given facilities at the Piedmontese port of Villafranca, near Nice.[1] In the next month Prince Napoleon had met the Tsar in Warsaw. It seemed that Russia was directly involved in the Italian plot, perhaps even allied formally with France and Piedmont. The English Government had overwhelming reason to try to prevent the fulfilment of Napoleon's plans, certainly by diplomatic, and perhaps by other, means.

On 7 January, in a dispatch which was 'so secret that the Prince Consort has begged me to keep it out of the office', Malmesbury told Prussia, then the Power most closely associated with England, that his Government's policy if war unfortunately broke out would be 'neutrality at all events and as long as possible'. But England would do her utmost to prevent war, and she had hopes that a permanent settlement of the Italian Question could be peacefully achieved; she would consider sympathetically any proposals to that end, even including territorial redistribution in the centre of the peninsula.[2] Later came a barrage of dispatches in which Malmesbury officially informed the various Powers of as much of this policy as it was good for each of them to know, that of 10 January to Cowley in Paris—what Malmesbury called his '*great* despatch'—and those of 12 January to Hudson in Turin, Lord Augustus Loftus in Vienna, Sir John Crampton in St Petersburg and Lord Bloomfield in Berlin. France, Piedmont and Austria were urged to caution: war would not solve the Italian Question and might well, either by strengthening Austrian influence or substituting French,

---

[1] W. E. Mosse, 'The Russians at Villafranca', *Slavonic Review*, vol. xxx (1952), pp. 425–43
[2] The dispatch is in RA J. 14. See 7 January, Malmesbury to Cowley (CP F.O. 519/196), cited partially in Earl of Malmesbury, *Memoirs of an Ex-Minister* (London, 1885, 1-vol. ed.), p. 457 and (undated) in Hon. F. A. Wellesley, *The Paris Embassy During the Second Empire* (London, 1928), p. 173.

make its solution more difficult ; war might promote revolution, which neither side could desire ; negotiation was the only satisfactory means of ameliorating the condition of Italy. As a beginning England suggested that the occupying troops of France and Austria should be withdrawn from the Papal State, and that the Powers should unite in encouraging the Pope to improve his régime. By contrast, Austria was congratulated on her administration in Lombardy. To Russia and Prussia Malmesbury merely wrote requesting assistance in mediation. He told all the Powers that England was impartial and would make every effort to preserve peace. But he attempted also to give to each of the probable belligerents a different impression of what England's policy would be in the event of war. Austria, who was not expected to risk even defensive war without allies, was assured that she would on no account receive English support against the cause of Italian liberty, and that England would definitely remain neutral ; while France, who would be content with English neutrality, was allowed to understand that England might oppose her.[1]

Malmesbury hoped by this deception both to exact concessions from Austria and to cool Napoleon's ardour, thereby settling the Italian Question and yet also preserving peace. That he failed ultimately was not for lack of expedients. When it became clear that the advice of January had had no effect, he sent Cowley to Vienna in late February with proposals which France appeared to sanction as a basis of agreement. Although the Treaties of 1815 were to be respected, the Papal State must be evacuated and reformed and—here Austria's other generally acknowledged usurpation of power

[1] *Correspondence relating to the Affairs of Italy, January to May 1859* (State Papers. Session 31 May–13 August 1859. Vol. xxxii. Command Paper No. 2524) [referred to as *Correspondence* in this and the next chapter], pp. 4–10. Malmesbury, *Memoirs*, p. 459

in Italy was assailed—the treaties promising assistance to some lesser Italian rulers against their subjects must be amended.[1] Cowley returned to Paris in the middle of March in the belief that Austria had given way, only to find that Russia, presumably in concert with France, had reopened every question by proposing a Congress on Italian affairs. It was well known that Austria preferred private negotiation to the publicity of a Congress, particularly as any European arrangement to pacify Italy was certain to be to her disadvantage. She now became thoroughly obstinate. She would not accept any reasonable scheme of representation for the Italian states in the Congress ; and either she or France rejected every plan for prior ' disarmament ', or demobilisation. Such verbal concessions as had been made were soon discovered to have no substance : Austria acquiesced in the modification of the obnoxious treaties only after advising the other signatories to insist on their continuance [2] ; and, although the Pope was persuaded to request the withdrawal of the forces occupying his State, and Malmesbury and Disraeli, the Chancellor of the Exchequer, announced to Parliament on 25 February the forthcoming evacuation, neither Power took the action which it had asserted its determination to take. For a brief moment, indeed, the Government believed it had attained its object : it at last prevailed upon France to bring pressure on Piedmont to agree that she would disarm if other Powers would do the same ; and this Piedmont most reluctantly did. But the surrender came too late to forestall an Austrian ultimatum sent on 19 April. Malmesbury wrote wearily to Cowley : ' we all from the Queen downwards thought the business was settled.' [3] Even then he persevered, appealing to the 23rd

[1] 22 February, Malmesbury to Cowley (*Correspondence*, pp. 54–5)
[2] F. Valsecchi, *La Mediazione Europea e la Definizione dell' Aggressore alla Vigilia della Guerra del 1859* (Rome, 1938), p. 34
[3] 20 April (CP F.O. 519/196)

protocol of the Treaty of Paris by which antagonistic Powers were exhorted to submit to mediation. But the task was now quite hopeless.

' While Cavour and Napoleon had a cause for war, but no excuse, the British Government had to make out that there were excuses, but no cause.' [1] It persisted in maintaining that the difficulties were entirely due to ' mutual faults of temper and indiscretion on the part of the two Governments '.[2] Though it recognised that the Italians had legitimate grievances, it denied the existence of an Italian problem that could not be settled by peaceful means, and tried to keep the question of reforms distinct from the international question. As far as the latter was concerned, it put the blame squarely on Piedmont :

> It is impossible, indeed, for any impartial person to agree with Count Cavour in seeking to justify the military preparations of Sardinia by the menacing attitude assumed by Austria. If the attitude of Austria imposes on Sardinia the present necessity, the language and conduct of Sardinia are, in the opinion of Her Majesty's Government, chiefly to blame for that attitude.[3]

There was some criticism of Austria. But, as *The Times* wrote when the Blue Book appeared : ' Lord Malmesbury adopts here and there a tenderness of expostulation in his remonstrances with Austria which is not to be found in the objurgations addressed to Sardinia.' [4]

In his private letters Malmesbury's language was much more violent than in his official dispatches. He wrote to Cowley on 13 January, for instance :

> France having always been a curse to Europe, we look upon it as the will of God, and resign ourselves to the torment, but . . .

---

[1] A. J. P. Taylor, *The Struggle for Mastery in Europe 1848–1918* (Oxford, 1954), p. 109   [2] *Correspondence*, p. 5
[3] 12 February, Malmesbury to Hudson (*ibid.* p. 45)   [4] 20 June

that Europe should be deluged with blood for the personal ambition of an Italian attorney and a tambour-major, like Cavour and his master, is intolerable.[1]

During the course of the negotiations Malmesbury came to the conclusion that France and Piedmont were chiefly responsible for the frustration of England's efforts to preserve peace : Napoleon appeared to have engineered the Congress proposal to destroy Cowley's achievements at Vienna ; Cavour would not at first promise, as Austria did, not to open hostilities ; and the Emperor refused, after initially agreeing, to join in a guarantee to Piedmont if she disarmed. When Cowley discovered that Napoleon intended this breach of faith, he told him on 8 April that :

if he [Napoleon] attempted, without reason, any scheme so iniquitous [as trying to drive Austria out of Italy], he would have both the moral and material efforts of England arrayed against him. . . . If H. M. wanted to unite Great Britain as one man against him he had only to take the course he had hinted at.

Malmesbury read Cowley's account of this incident to the Cabinet, and reported that ' they all agreed that you did not say a word too much to the man who broke his word to you, and who it is evident to me has from the first meant an Italian war.' [2]

Malmesbury himself always denied that his Government's policy had favoured Austria ; and several points can be made in its defence. Count Buol, the Austrian Foreign Minister, was definitely not satisfied with England's attitude. He described Malmesbury's hints about territorial redistribution in Central Italy ' as a most dangerous doctrine, and as subversive of the

---

[1] CP F.O. 519/196, printed undated in Wellesley, *The Paris Embassy*, p. 175
[2] Wellesley, *The Paris Embassy*, pp. 179–81. See also *Correspondence*, pp. 133, 172, 186, 234 and 247, and Malmesbury, *Memoirs*, pp. 474–5

Treaties of 1815 '.[1] Though the Government was very critical of France, and more especially of Piedmont, it never ranged itself explicitly with Austria. In fact it refused to guarantee Austria against Piedmontese aggression,[2] although it was willing to participate in a joint guarantee with France of Piedmont against Austrian aggression. Malmesbury was known as, and regarded himself as, a promoter of the French alliance, having restored good relations with Napoleon after the Orsini crisis.[3] Furthermore, if he had persuaded the Powers to go into Congress, he would probably have argued strongly for substantial changes in Italy. He considered himself decidedly pro-Italian ; and he intended to take to the meeting Hudson, who was a personal friend, as his ' Italian encyclopaedia '.[4]

There can be no doubt, however, that he and his Government, though well intentioned, seriously misjudged the situation. Not only did they altogether fail to understand the Piedmontese approach to the Italian Question. They also failed to appreciate properly that Austria was prepared to fight for her rights in Italy, preferring as she did the possibility— even the probability—of defeat in war to the certainty of defeat at the conference-table. They were much quicker to believe Austrian than French assurances ; and Malmesbury remarked that, while he tried to *compel* Piedmont to be moderate, he only *asked* Austria.[5] Even though Austria gave warning that she would request Piedmont to disarm, the English Government continued to rely on her 'spirit of dignified conciliation'.[6]

[1] 20 January, Loftus to Malmesbury (*Correspondence*, p. 23)
[2] *Correspondence*, p. 208 ; 4 March, Malmesbury to Cowley (RA J. 16/12) ; and Hearder, *Rass. stor. del Ris.*, vol. xliii (1956), pp. 53–4
[3] Malmesbury, *Memoirs*, pp. 417–24
[4] Massari, *Diario*, p. 194 (under 7 April). Lacaita, *An Italian Englishman*, pp. 259–60
[5] 15 February, 29 March, 4 April, to Cowley (CP F.O. 519/196)
[6] Disraeli, in *Parl. Deb.*, 3rd series, vol. cliii, col. 1869 (18 April). *Correspondence*, pp. 246–7

If the Conservative Ministers were not biased, they were unquestionably blinkered.

Whether England could have hoped to avert a war for which both France and Austria were ready must remain doubtful. It seems clear that she could not conceivably have done so except by committing herself decisively to one side or the other. It appears that this possibility was not contemplated until, at the last moment, on 21 April, the Cabinet discussed a suggestion that ' England should threaten to come to the aid of Sardinia, if the contemplated invasion should take place'. But the Cabinet were not ' prepared to take so strong a step, which would commit them to measures to which they might be unable at the moment to give due effect ; and which, if Austria were to disregard the measure, would involve them in War as the Allies of France '.[1]

II

Very little evidence is available relating to the formation of the Conservative Government's policy at Cabinet level, whether before or after the Austrian ultimatum. It is clear that the Cabinet was summoned to settle the broad lines, and at important moments. From Derby's letters to the Queen it is plain that he superintended Malmesbury's work ; as Prime Minister, and as by far the most experienced and the best-known figure in the Cabinet, he naturally exerted great influence.[2] Disraeli, since he was Leader of the House, had to defend the Government's policy, and had therefore a right to be carefully consulted. He is found writing to the Prime Minister criticising Malmesbury for idleness, ignorance

[1] 21 April, Derby to the Queen (*QVL*, vol. iii, p. 327)
[2] There are many more of these letters in RA J. 14–19 and A. 27 than would be suspected from *QVL*.

and indecision.[1] He derived from his unofficial and unreliable contacts in Paris a low opinion of Cowley's ability and a rosy view of Napoleon's intentions, both of which he confided to Derby.[2] After the event at least, he put much of the blame for the failure to restrain Austria on Loftus, 'a pompous nincompoop, and of all Lord Malmesbury's appointments the worst; and that is saying a good deal'.[3] But at the time he shared the misapprehensions of the rest of the Cabinet about the Italian Question and about Austria's attitude[4]; and there is no ground for supposing that he wished for a policy very different from that which Derby and Malmesbury desired. Of the influence of other members of the Cabinet, and even of their views, there is no trace. It is dangerous to come to a conclusion on mainly negative evidence. But it is certain that there were over foreign policy no disputes so violent as those which were to trouble Palmerston's Ministry; and it seems probable that there were no fundamental disagreements. Perhaps the Cabinet was too busy dividing over the question of Parliamentary Reform, on which two Ministers resigned.

Of individuals outside the Cabinet, the Queen and Cowley were the most influential. Until April the Queen made few attempts to modify the Government's policy, because it accorded so well with her own opinions. Royal interference, as will appear in the next Chapter, became much more frequent after the beginning of the war. Throughout the Conservative Ministry Cowley was Malmesbury's chief adviser and informant, and his most trusted envoy. He was

[1] 4 and 7 January : [W. F. Monypenny &] G. E. Buckle, *The Life of Benjamin Disraeli* (London, 1910–20), vol. iv, pp. 221–2
[2] *ibid.* pp. 216–28. See G. B. Henderson, 'Ralph Anstruther Earle', *English Historical Review*, vol. lviii (1943), pp. 172–89
[3] Buckle, *Disraeli*, vol. iv, p. 228 ('written in the sixties')
[4] 4 January, Disraeli to Derby, and 19 April, to Mrs Brydges Willyams (*ibid.* vol. iv, pp. 221, 214)

allowed considerable discretion in his dealings with the Emperor, and was also employed to sound the English Opposition leaders, with whom he sympathised in domestic politics. The Foreign Secretary himself described the Blue Book on Italian affairs, published in June, as their joint work.[1]

Something should be said about Hudson, who, though he was very well placed to exert influence, does not seem to have done so. Malmesbury was intending to take him to the Congress ; but he was also trying to remove him from Turin.[2] The Foreign Secretary was shocked to learn that Cavour regarded Hudson as ultra ' Italian ' ; and he was thoroughly indignant to discover that his Minister to Piedmont had been disclosing to Cavour the contents of some highly confidential dispatches, among which was that of 12 January to Loftus stating definitely that England would remain neutral if war broke out.[3] Malmesbury, however, was ' hampered by the rule, become general since I was last in office, that no change can be made without the approbation of the Ministers themselves '[4] ; and he did not succeed in arranging an exchange between Hudson and another envoy before the Government fell. It may be that, because of his personal friendship with Hudson, the Foreign Secretary was glad enough to encounter these difficulties. But it seems evident that Hudson's pro-Piedmontese despatches were ignored in London as hopelessly prejudiced : Malmesbury wrote of him to Cowley that ' I never saw a man even in English politics so besotted by the peculiar bias of opinion.'[5]

[1] Wellesley, *The Paris Embassy*, pp. 171–83, esp. p. 183
[2] 3 March and 7 June, Malmesbury to the Queen (RA J. 16/6 and B. 17/131)
[3] *The Greville Memoirs*, vol. viii, p. 282 ; 29 March (CP F.O. 519/196). 28 February, Malmesbury to the Prince Consort (RA J. 15/109) ; Massari, *Diario*, p. 120 (19 January) and *passim* ; *CC Ing.*, vol. ii, part i, p. 275
[4] 29 March, to Cowley (CP F.O. 519/196) [5] 9 June (*ibid.*)

III

To make possible a study of the ' Italian ' issue in the party struggle of 1859, it is necessary to consider in some detail the early stages of the Parliamentary and public reaction to the crisis. That done, an attempt will be made to assess the influence of Parliament and the public on the Conservatives' foreign policy up to the Austrian ultimatum.

Napoleon and Cavour had expected that the very nature of their policy would ensure English popular backing. Disraeli, in an important letter of 7 January to Derby, from a deeper knowledge of English feeling, suggested another possibility :

> Next to, or perhaps equal with, his desire ' to do something for Italy ' is the Emperor's wish—I might say passion—to restore the good opinion of the English people in his favor. For this he is prepared to make great sacrifices, to force free trade in France, perhaps even to reduce his marine.
>
> At this moment he is meditating a great rhetorical *coup*. . . . His Chambers, or whatever they are called, meet early in February. He will seize that opportunity . . . of taking a view of public affairs, and he will make a great effort to put himself right with England. *Mind, England*, not the *English Ministry*, though we shall be blunderers if we permit the present estrangement to continue.
>
> Now, observe : there are two things at this conjuncture most urgent. First, to impress upon Austria that, in the event of war between her and France, England will not interfere. . . . Austria is unwilling to believe this. . . . But if Austria is convinced that we shall be neutral, then she will be conciliatory, and she would agree to a revival of the Conferences at Paris to consider the condition of Central and Southern Italy. This overture on her part would enlist English opinion on her side, and on English opinion at this moment everything depends.
>
> The Emperor is watching it with intenseness, down to an article

in the *Daily News*. He will never risk a war which England dis-
approves. If opinion here sanction the conciliatory movement of
Austria, he will . . . content himself with a diplomatic triumph.[1]

Although excessively optimistic about the attitudes of both
Napoleon and Austria, this letter shows a sound grasp of the
English situation and demonstrates now much the Government took public opinion into account. Malmesbury acted
on the same assumptions as Disraeli here revealed. He warned
Prussia that English opinion must in the normal way be
expected to favour Italy; he therefore advised Austria to be
amenable in order to counteract this tendency; and he further
assured France that English opinion would swing against
whichever side should be the aggressor.[2]

While Malmesbury wrote, the reaction to Napoleon's
remark of New Year's Day was verifying this last prediction.
France appeared plainly as a would-be aggressor and English
opinion at once turned against her. ' The alarm in the City '
was ' very great '; Malmesbury thought ' the panic may do
good, and let the worst come to the worst it's rather pleasant
to see the Bulls head turned the other way and looking South
instead of North.' [3] *The Times* felt it ' need not enlarge on
the grossness of the artifice which seeks, after so many years,
to palm upon us the Emperor Louis Napoleon as the enemy
of any abuse however inveterate, or the champion of any
reform however necessary.' [4] The Queen told King Leopold
of the Belgians that the framing of her Speech at the opening
of Parliament had been difficult, ' as the feeling *against* the
Emperor here is *very strong* '.[5] Of the Press, practically only the

---

[1] Buckle, *Disraeli*, vol. iv, pp. 223–4
[2] 7 January, to Bloomfield (RA J. 14). 12 January, to Loftus (*Correspondence*, p. 8). 11 January, to Cowley (Malmesbury, *Memoirs*, p. 458)
[3] 14 January, Disraeli to Derby (Buckle, *Disraeli*, vol. iv, p. 225). **13**
January, Malmesbury to Cowley (CP F.O. 519/196) [4] 10 January
[5] 2 February (Q*VL*, vol. iii, p. 314)

Morning Post, once Palmerstonian but now positively Bonapartist, expressed trust in Napoleon ; and the *Daily News* was almost equally unusual in its qualified optimism : the remainder, whether Conservative or Liberal, anticipated no good from a French invasion of Italy, which could only end with ' Freedom in ashes '.[1] On this point even the Mazzinians agreed with the country as a whole.[2] Public opinion distrusted French professions of disinterest quite as much as did the Government. It seemed impossible that Napoleon, the pillar of the Catholic and absolutist Reaction, could honestly mean to free Italy.

Peace was the universal desire ; the English refused to see any respectable ground for war. In consequence Piedmont's previous popularity dwindled, giving way to ' *universal ill-will against Italy* '.[3] *The Times*, for example, marked its displeasure by discontinuing a series of articles by the great Italian federalist, Carlo Cattaneo. [4] As Azeglio wrote :

Here in England this whole phantasmagoria has appeared unexpectedly, and, as people know little either of our anti-German instincts or of the part that we are called upon to play as representatives of an Italian idea, they cannot resist the idea that we are either hare-brained or Don Quixotes.[5]

As late as 15 March he reported that ' in all sorts of ways we are losing ground in public opinion, even among the Liberals, who regard us as men of unbridled ambition.' [6] English-

[1] For Press opinion in this phase see M. B. Urban, *British Opinion and Policy on the Unification of Italy, 1856–1861* (Scottdale, Pa., U.S.A., 1938), chs. iv–v. *Newcastle Guardian*, 15 January
[2] J. L. & B. Hammond, *James Stansfeld* (London, 1932), p. 39 ; *Scritti di Mazzini*, vol. lxiii, p. 144
[3] 8 February (Brooks, *Panizzi*, p. 231)
[4] ed. R. Caddeo, *Epistolario di Carlo Cattaneo* (Florence, 1949–56), vol. iii, pp. 91*n* and 95*n*
[5] 24 January, to his mother : ed. A. Colombo, *Carteggi e Documenti Diplomatici inediti di Emanuele d'Azeglio*, vol. ii (' non ultimato, edizione fuori commercio '), p. 178   [6] *CC Ing.*, vol. ii, part i, p. 278

men entirely failed to sympathise with the attitude of the Piedmontese to the Italian problem : Malmesbury's blindness was typical. No doubt there would have arisen still more violent antagonism to France and Piedmont if there had not been widespread support for Italian liberty ; but such support as there was did not gratify Cavourians.

Should war break out, public opinion pronounced firmly for neutrality. Newspapers of whatever hue, by whatever reasoning, arrived at the recommendation that in a conflict between two despots, from which only harm was likely to accrue, England must stand aside. The English felt sure that neither side could be trusted. It is incontestable that Malmesbury's policy, in its broad lines, commanded general approval, at least in the first three months of 1859.

Parliament met at the beginning of February. Napoleon was waiting ' to see how the cat jumped ' there. But he could derive no comfort from the attitude of the Opposition leaders.[1] Both Palmerston and Russell proved extremely moderate. Palmerston in private maintained that ' the Austrians have no business in Italy, and they are a public nuisance there ; ' but he admitted that Austria's retirement from Italy, though ' an unmixed good ', ' would be too dearly bought by the calamities and dangers of such a war as would be necessary for its accomplishment.' If war broke out, ' We must stand aloof. Public opinion would not allow the Government to declare war against France, Sardinia and Russia, in order to maintain Austria in Italy, and of course it is out of the question that we should take part against Austria.'[2] Palmerston's special

---

[1] 9 February, Granville to Canning : Lord Edmond Fitzmaurice, *The Life of Second Earl Granville* (London, 1905), vol. i, p. 324. 6 February, Cowley to Malmesbury (*QVL*, vol. iii, p. 317). cf. Sir T. Martin, *The Life of H.R.H. the Prince Consort* (London, 1875–80), pp. 384–5

[2] 30 January, to Granville (Fitzmaurice, *Granville*, vol. i, pp. 325–6). **End** of January, to Cowley (Wellesley, *The Paris Embassy*, pp. 174–5)

concern had long been the French alliance. Russell was more particularly interested in Italy. But even he was talking of the possibility that England might have to go to war to maintain Austria as a Great Power if Vienna itself was threatened. Otherwise she must remain neutral, as :

> The question could not arise in a worse shape. The most prominent fact is the occupation of the Roman States by France & Austria, & in the face of this fact the Pope's bad Govt. is to be sustained by foreign force while Piedmont is to be enlarged and aggrandized.[1]

Clarendon, the previous Foreign Secretary and expected to become the next one, although he had acquired a considerable reputation for Italian sympathies by his attacks on Austria at the Congress of Paris, and although he had been as insistent as anyone that 'Bomba' should be ostracised, was now less favourable than formerly towards Piedmont ; and he was a determined enemy of French intervention.[2] He influenced Palmerston and Russell to be moderate in their public utterances. But he thought the trend of public opinion was the best guarantee of that. He analysed the situation for Cowley on 2 February :

> Austria is so unpopular here & there is so much sympathy with Italian hatred of her rule that people don't like to say all they think for fear of being considered *Austrian* otherwise the explosion of opinion about the conduct of France & of Piedmont as her instrument wd be ten times louder than it is, but the distrust of the Empr. & the change of public opinion with respect to him are complete & will be lasting. I look to the debate in Pt. tomorrow with much anxiety but with more hope than I did a fortnight ago—the indignation wch prevails in London & all the

---

[1] 26 December 1858, to Clarendon : ed. G. P. Gooch, *Later Correspondence of Lord John Russell* (London, 1925), vol. ii, p. 229. 27 December, to the Dean of Bristol (RP PRO 30/22/13)
[2] 24 December, Clarendon to Russell (*ibid.*)

great towns has had its effect & it is clear that political capital wd be lost and not made by a warlike tone or by sympathy in Italian grievances pushed to its extreme limits. I have had long conversations with Palmn & Ld John & altho their anti Austn feelings are strong & their desire is first to see Austria removed from Italy yet I think that they will speak prudently & moderately.[1]

This hope was justified. And on 28 March he was still able to write :

I dare say the Emperor is speculating upon the change of Government, and the countenance he shall receive to his anti-Austrian policy from Palmerston and Lord John. He will be disappointed however, for at present no Minister could stand a week who was thought to be favourable to war.[2]

A slight shift of opinion occurred in late March and early April. Gladstone wrote a most perceptive account of it in an article in the *Quarterly Review*. At the beginning of the year he had been in the Ionian Islands on a special mission to consider how their constitution might be modified. On his return journey he passed through Austrian Italy and spent three days in Turin, dining with Cavour on 3 and 4 March.[3] Soon after reaching England he wrote to Hudson, on 14 March :

The feeling here is anti-Italian. Though I have never joined in the cry against the stranger as such, though I entirely mistrust every *nostrum* for Italy except that of local freedom, I find myself already booked even in high quarters as an *ultra* Italian. I wished to write or get something written, on the state of the political question as it now stands for Lombardy. But as far as I can yet find, both the great Reviews are closed against anything of the sort, under the notion of keeping peace. I am for peace as much as most men : but if we want to have steady peace in Italy, we must mend the conditions of existence. . . .

[1] CP F.O. 519/178
[2] *ibid.*, printed undated in Wellesley, *The Paris Embassy*, p. 179
[3] Massari, *Diario*, pp. 156–60

The English believe, as they are taught, that Austria stands wholly on the defensive, & that Piedmont wants to repeat the ruinous experiment of 1848. All effective sympathy for Piedmont is crushed as long as this belief prevails. . . .

I cannot blame her for her close relations with France. They are the inevitable result of our philo-Turkish fanaticism & close embraces with Austria. But this apology holds good only so long as they are purely defensive, & if, misled by dynastic & territorial ambition, Piedmont becomes an instrument for purposes of offence then it may be doubtful whether even her Constitution will survive the confusions that are to follow.[1]

In his article, completed in the middle of April and published early in May, he first described the reaction to Napoleon's *gaffe* :

A sentiment not unlike that which excited this country during the Russian war was enlisted on behalf of Austria. . . . We know not what may have been the views of our Government ; but, so far as the people were concerned, the course which opinion manifestly took after this announcement was not due to any love for the Austrian Government or system, but to mistrust of Louis Napoleon. . . .

So ' Italian interests were viewed in England, not as they are in themselves, but as the ministerial instruments of French or rather of Napoleonic ambition.' ' For us, a few weeks ago, there was no Italian question ; it was a phrase blazoned on a French banner, and it was nothing more. Sardinia was mentioned only to be condemned.'

Within the last few weeks, however, there has certainly been a change in the tone of English opinion and in some among its prominent though more ephemeral organs. Probably it may have dated from the appearance of that dispatch, which Count Buol on the 25th February addressed to the Austrian Minister in London. It was published early in March . . . [and] was calculated to

[1] GP BM Add MS 44391, f.206

produce far worse impressions than any attack from a hostile quarter. . . .

The dispatch was followed by the appearance of the second of the letters from Signor Farini to Lord John Russell . . ., by a masterly reply from Count Cavour, and by the more recent publication of the note of that statesman dated the 1st of March, in which, at the request of the British Minister, he sets forth what he thinks the essential and immediate requisites for the peace of Italy.

Gladstone goes on to demonstrate Austria's total rejection of compromise, her deleterious influence in Italy, her utter hatred of free institutions. She is not even, in claiming praise for her administration in Lombardy, 'entitled to measure her merits upwards from a standard, which she herself has mainly contributed to depress'. He does not, on the other hand, show much sympathy with Piedmont's motives of aggrandisement or with Italian nationalism, and he concludes :

The neutrality of England will in all likelihood be matter not of prudence only, but of the very highest moral obligation. The relief of Italy is an honourable end, but it must not be sought by unholy means. . . . The power of Austria is vital to the equilibrium of Europe : but we must not be parties to defending for the sake of that power the acts and maxims by which she has been the means of inflicting beyond the Alps such woes on mankind. If we cannot assist Louis Napoleon without the fear of promoting piracy, so neither can we help Austria without the certainty of becoming the tools of tyranny.[1]

According to the diarist, Greville, Gladstone had been 'completely duped by Cavour'; but to the Piedmontese themselves his article seemed not to have touched the real question.[2] All that he, and others who sympathised with

[1] Q.R., vol. cv (1859), quotations from pp. 531, 532, 537, 537–8, 558 and 563
[2] The Greville Memoirs, vol. viii, p. 236 (24 March). Massari, Diario, p. 237 (11 May)

him, aimed to do was to forestall what they saw as a pressing danger, an English alliance with Austria. The comparison with 1854 had occurred to other people. Aberdeen, for example, thought there was at least as much justification for war against France, if she invaded Italy, as there had been for England's participation in the Crimean War.[1] On this occasion, however, the fear of the current bogy could be counteracted to some extent by educing pro-Italian sentiment. Feeling remained strongly anti-French, but hardened against Austria and softened in favour of Piedmont. English opinion began to justify Cavour's intransigence in the face of Austrian bullying, even if it still disapproved of his going to war. The *Daily News* remarked that there was more agreement with its anti-Austrian attitude than at any time since December; the *Saturday Review* began to talk of the need to take into account English sympathy with the Italians; and *The Times*, from Monday, 4 April, adopted a friendlier tone.[2] One of the factors in this alteration of Press opinion was the visit to London of Emanuele Marliani, a supporter of Cavour and a friend of Clarendon. He had encouraging talks with prominent statesmen and his ' conversation with Delane [the editor of *The Times*] produced the remarkable article . . . of Monday last wch has had an indescribable effect here by directing public opinion here to something that is practical & that consequently is not war or the abrogation of Treaties.'[3] A month earlier Delane had wished, while the Neapolitan prisoners released by ' Bomba ' were being fêted in London,

---

[1] Parker, *Graham*, vol. ii, pp. 374–5
[2] *Daily News*, 11 April. *Saturday Review*, 9 April
[3] 7 April, Clarendon to Cowley (CP F.O. 519/178). See 4 April, Delane to Panizzi : Panizzi MSS, BM Add MS 36719, quoted in *The History of ' The Times '*, vol. ii, p. 332. And 5 April, Clarendon to Reeve, *ibid.* p. 331*n*
For the talks with statesmen see *CC Ing.*, vol. ii, part i, pp. 288–98 ; 5 April, Clarendon to Russell (RP PRO 30/22/13) ; *The Greville Memoirs*, vol. viii pp. 238–9.

that ' we could do enough for them to prove that though we deprecate a war between France and Austria on very ill-defined grounds we can still sympathise cordially with Italian patriotism '.[1] At that time Azeglio had had to remain in the background owing to the general condemnation of Piedmont, merely hoping that some advantage to the Italian cause might result from the reception.[2] Now there was more goodwill. It was beginning to be appreciated that Austria was extremely obstructive, perhaps even that she might be contemplating aggression. Nevertheless, the original distrust of war and of French aggrandisement was still present : Marliani had only obtained his success by appearing to have ' as great a horror of war as John Bright affects to have '.[3] Moreover, the revived sympathy for Italy was still associated with an inadequate understanding of the Italian Question ; and evidently it would not persist unless fortunate circumstances or consummate skill should enable Cavour to pose for Englishmen as an aggrieved party on the defensive against the enemies of constitutionalism.

So in April, while the Government, as Malmesbury's letters to Cowley show, was becoming increasingly incensed against France, public opinion was inclining against Austria. Some divergence was revealed in the Parliamentary debates of 18 April. Not only did Derby claim that Austria was constant in her declarations, but he also alluded to the necessity that England should arm even though she must try to remain neutral ; and he remarked ominously : ' even for this country it would be impossible to look with total indifference at any alteration of the occupation of the shores of the Adriatic.' Disraeli made similar comments to the Lower House.[4] Though

[1] Delane to Shaftesbury, reported on 10 March by Azeglio to Cavour' (CC Ing., vol. ii, part i, p. 266)   [2] 8 March, to Cavour (ibid. p. 263)
[3] 7 April, Clarendon to Cowley (CP F.O. 519/178)
[4] Parl. Deb., 3rd series, vol. cliii, cols. 1830–57 and 1863–97 ; the quotation from col. 1856

to Greville the striking feature of these speeches, and of Clarendon's for the Opposition, was 'their reticence and forbearance about France' as compared with the treatment meted out to the Tsar in 1854,[1] to the Liberals the threat of intervention, however remote, was now entirely repugnant. Gladstone spoke for many when he denied Austria's constancy; and he and Palmerston both suggested that Piedmont, in being asked to disarm, was not being fairly treated. The Foreign Secretary could not help noticing 'a very strong Sardinian feeling in the House of Commons & nothing is required to make it blaze forth but the smallest act of injustice by Austria'.[2] The Liberal statesmen, in fact, were privately less sanguine about the Conservatives' policy than they were in public: Clarendon recognised that 'Austria *does* require some pressure;' Russell trusted neither side, thinking, 'they are all waiting for an occasion to say "You see the war was not my fault";' and Palmerston had foreseen the possibility that Austria might attack Piedmont as soon as Cavour disarmed.[3] There were already the makings of a foreign-policy issue between the parties.

IV

As a minority Government, the Conservative Administration was specially vulnerable in the House of Commons; and, to the outside world, the views of the Opposition leaders, who would be likely to succeed to power before very long, might well seem more important than those of Ministers. The Government's prestige sank very low after its defeat on

[1] *The Greville Memoirs*, vol. viii, p. 242
[2] 20 April, Malmesbury to Cowley (CP F.O. 519/196)
[3] 5 April, Clarendon to Reeve (*History of 'The Times'*, vol. ii, p. 331n). 21 April, Russell to Clarendon (Bodleian MS Clar. dep. c.104). 15 April, Palmerston to Clarendon (*ibid.* c. 529)

31 March in the House of Commons over Parliamentary Reform. Malmesbury was very conscious of the weakness of his position, as his *Memoirs* show[1]; and he did what he could to remedy it by keeping in touch with Palmerston and Clarendon, in the hope of persuading them to be moderate in their public statements.[2] Parliament, however, can have exerted little direct influence on his policy. It did not meet until after the formative period was over. When it did meet, it was mainly occupied with Reform. The House of Lords was in any case very Conservative in foreign policy; and the House of Commons proved remarkably tolerant of the Government's jejune pronouncements, even when they had been several times deferred on the plea that delicate negotiations were in progress. No demands were made for the production of papers. In general, the debates on foreign policy must have assisted Malmesbury to pursue his chosen line, by displaying such a wide measure of agreement between the two parties. On the other hand, it was plainly an embarrassment to the Government to make statements on 18 April, which they could hardly escape doing since that was the last effective day of the Parliament.

To determine the influence of public opinion is by no means easy. It must first be recognised that, although the public can often be kept very well informed by the Press about the progress of a revolution or a war abroad, during a purely diplomatic crisis the facts about Governments' policies, on which alone a worth-while judgment can be founded, are seldom immediately available. Hence the importance in these months of *The Times*, which was known to be favoured with confidential information by Cabinet Ministers; the impor-

[1] e.g. pp. 458, 471, 485
[2] Wellesley, *The Paris Embassy*, pp. 173-4; 4 March, the Queen to Malmesbury, and 5 March, Malmesbury to the Queen (RA J. 16); 10 April, Malmesbury to Palmerston (BMS)

tance of their Parliamentary pronouncements ; and the importance of the few dispatches that were published, unofficially.[1] The Conservatives, controlling the executive, had the initiative; and they had the opportunity to frame a policy in a situation which might be expected to daunt the Liberal leaders. Not only was the Opposition divided ; but Russell had been out of office for four years because he had mismanaged a negotiation with Austria during the Crimean War ; and Palmerston and Clarendon had been turned out for showing consideration to the French Emperor in the previous February. The Government had every inducement to try to make its policy popular. On a question of such importance a Blue Book would eventually have to be published. Before then, statements would have to be made in Parliament. And, though at the beginning of the session the Liberals were still disunited in the House of Commons, it was probable that there would be a reconciliation, that the Conservatives would be defeated, and that a General Election would follow. Moreover, foreign Governments would be more inclined to pay heed to the words of a weak Ministry if it were obviously backed by public opinion. There is no doubt that the Cabinet took all these considerations into account. This is evident from Disraeli's letter, already quoted, from Malmesbury's correspondence with Cowley, and from his dispatches.[2] But of course the influence of opinion could be only of a general character, especially since Ministers' calculations had to be based on their predictions of popular reactions to the developing crisis. It would seem that for the moment the Government was restrained from showing deeper

[1] *History of 'The Times'*, vol. ii, esp. chs. xii and xvi and pp. 327–8 ; A. I' Dasent, *The Life of J. T. Delane* (London, 1908), vol. i, pp. 307–08. Gladstone' Q.R., vol. cv (1859), pp. 537–8 ; 15 April, Palmerston to Clarendon (Bodleian MS Clar. dep. c.529). See *CC Ing.*, vol. ii, part i, esp. pp. 273–4, 291–2, 296 and 298–300

[2] Disraeli to Derby (Buckle, *Disraeli*, vol. iv, pp. 223–4) ; Malmesbury, *Memoirs*, p. 471, and CP F.O. 519/196 ; *Correspondence*, pp. 8, 170, 191, etc.

sympathy with Austria by pro-Italian feeling, but that it was counting on a strengthening of anti-French sentiment in the future. On 4 March Malmesbury, while making it clear that England could not guarantee Austria, went on to say : ' every Liberal act of Austria will prepare the Public Mind here to resist Aggression hereafter.' [1] A month later he told Cowley the Government must be ready ' to stand clear before the public of the rascality going on at Paris. You must take care where you have not done so to cover yr Telegrams by despatches. I want to put on record that Austria is justified & that we have been deceived by France.' [2] It might be thought that Malmesbury exaggerated the potential strength of anti-French feeling. But, in view of the Orsini crisis and the panic of 1860, this seems improbable. He misjudged the European, rather than the domestic, situation. On the whole his policy proved popular in these months, for the public shared most of his misconceptions.

[1] To Cowley (RA J. 16/12)   [2] 4 April (CP F.O. 519/196)

Chapter IV

The War, the General Election and the Change of Government

19 April to mid-June 1859

MALMESBURY's final attempt at mediation was rejected before the end of April, and during May the war began in earnest. Napoleon announced his determination to free Italy from the Alps to the Adriatic. He won two great victories in June, at Magenta and Solferino; and in the first week of July he seemed on the point of fulfilling his declared mission. Under cover of the war, moreover, risings occurred in Tuscany, Modena, Parma and the Romagna, in all of which pro-Piedmontese provisional governments were established by mid-June. At that moment not only Lombardy and Venetia but also much of Central Italy appeared to be well on the way to independence.

I

The English Government's verbal reaction to the news of Austria's ultimatum was violent. Lord Derby publicly described her action as 'criminal'. An official protest was sent, and Austria was informed that she 'forfeits all claim upon the support or sympathy of England.' [1] Malmesbury

[1] *The Times*, 26 April. 21 April, Malmesbury to Loftus (*Correspondence*, p. 276)

told Cowley that he thought England would finally have to join France in defence of Piedmont, ' even if Palmerston or John Russell do not turn us out ' ! [1] Less than a fortnight after threatening Napoleon that England would fight France, Cowley found himself threatening the Austrian Ambassador in Paris that she would fight Austria.[2]

For the present, however, having protested, England showed her displeasure merely by ostentatiously abandoning her role of mediator, and by avowing herself strictly, passively, neutral.[3] A proclamation was issued forbidding British subjects to participate in the struggle in any way.[4]

Of course it was not to be expected that an attitude of total resignation would be maintained. The Government continued to deploy the influence of England in order to localise the war. The neutral Powers were enjoined to prudence. Before the outbreak of war the Government's wish to preserve peace had dictated pressure on France. Now its desire to prevent the conflict spreading compelled pressure on other Powers, which would redound principally to the advantage of France. As Prince Albert wrote :

The *mot d'ordre* from Paris, which is echoed from Petersburg, is *localiser la guerre*, and it sounds thoroughly humane and philan-thropic. But its real meaning is, Europe, and particularly Germany, are to sit still and look on, while France beats Austria in Italy and deprives her of her Italian provinces, tears up the Treaties of 1815, and shapes Italy to her liking and makes her dependent upon herself. . . . Russia seeks an alliance with England *pour localiser la guerre*, and there are some here who like the idea. . . .[5]

The Queen frustrated that proposal ; but Malmesbury was

[1] 20 April (CP F.O. 519/196)
[2] 21 April, Cowley to Malmesbury (RA J. 18/28)
[3] *Correspondence*, p. 234 etc.
[4] *The Times*, 13 May. See ed. Jagow, *Letters of the Prince Consort*, pp. 332–3 [5] 25 May, to the Prince Regent of Prussia (*ibid.* p. 334)

allowed to urge repeatedly on the German states, and also on Naples, the perils of intervention.[1]

There were, on the other hand, many matters on which England seemed to take a pro-Austrian line. France had already been warned that she should not try to establish herself on the Adriatic. By the end of April the existence of an alliance between France and Russia was regarded as certain. So Russia was warned not to interfere with the neutralisation of the Baltic.[2] With respect to developments in the Italian peninsula, Malmesbury based himself on the principle that the *status quo ante bellum* must be treated as the lawful situation. He therefore refused to recognise the provisional governments of Central Italy, treating them as puppets of Piedmont. He also took the opportunity of the death of ' Bomba ' on 22 May to open negotiations with Naples for the resumption of normal diplomatic relations, broken off in 1856.[3]

Thus the Government was putting itself in a somewhat equivocal position. Despite its original protest against the ultimatum, it was in theory supporting many of the contentions of Austria. But it now had no idea of assisting her effectively. And in practice its neutrality and its efforts at localisation were playing into the hands of Napoleon and Cavour.

II

Austria's ultimatum caused a revulsion of public feeling also. The Queen was in despair :

[1] *QVL*, vol. iii, pp. 334–5 ; *Correspondence*, p. 377 and *passim* ; 31 May, Malmesbury to Cowley (CP F.O. 519/196)

[2] H. W. V. Temperley & L. M. Penson, *Foundations of British Foreign Policy* (Cambridge, 1938), pp. 201–02 ; Malmesbury, *Memoirs*, p. 482

[3] *Further Correspondence respecting the Affairs of Italy* (State Papers. Session 31 May–13 August 1859. Vol. xxxii. Command Paper No. 2527), pp. 23, 64, 101–02, 103 and *passim*. See CC Ing., vol. ii, part i, pp. 334–5

I hardly know what to say. . . . Though it is *originally* the wicked folly of Russia and France that have brought about this fearful crisis, it is the madness and blindness of Austria which have brought on the war *now* ! It has put *them* in the wrong, and entirely changed the feeling here, which was all that one could desire, into the most *vehement* sympathy for *Sardinia*.[1]

It was reported to Cavour that Piedmont's ' position in opinion has profited and improves every day.' [2] Moreover, the virtually bloodless revolutions in Central Italy evoked great admiration : this was what Englishmen had always hoped for.[3] By mid-May Clarendon could not deny that ' a good deal of anti Austr steam is rising in the country.' [4]

Yet, although Austria's action disposed of the possibility that public opinion would support intervention against France at this stage, and released pent-up feelings of sympathy with Italian Liberals, it did not, save for a few days, diminish the force of anti-French sentiment. The animosity was soon revived by the rumours, assiduously propagated by *The Times*, of a Franco-Russian alliance. A serious panic on the Stock Exchange followed the first articles on 27 and 28 April.[5] The publication of Tennyson's poem ' Riflemen form ! ' in *The Times* of 9 May may be taken to mark the moment when the Volunteer Rifle Club Movement caught the public imagination. It also expresses very well the dominant mood :

> There is a sound of thunder afar,
> Storm in the South that darkens the day !
> Storm of battle and thunder of war !
> Well if it do not roll our way.
> Storm, Storm, Riflemen form !

[1] 26 April, to King Leopold (*QVL*, vol. iii, p. 328)
[2] 22 April, M. d'Azeglio to Cavour (*CC Ing.*, vol. ii, part i, p. 316)
[3] See Urban, *British Opinion and Policy*, ch. vii, esp. pp. 212–13
[4] 12 May, to Cowley (CP F.O. 519/196)
[5] *The Economist*, 30 April

Ready, be ready against the storm !
Riflemen, Riflemen, Riflemen form !

Be not deaf to the sound that warns,
Be not gull'd by a despot's plea !
Are figs of thistles ? or grapes of thorns ?
How can a despot feel with the Free ?
Form, Form, Riflemen Form !
Ready, be ready to meet the storm !
Riflemen, Riflemen, Riflemen form !

Let your reforms for a moment go !
Look to your butts, and take good aims !
Better a rotten borough or so
Than a rotten fleet and a city in flames !
Storm, Storm, Riflemen form !
Ready, be ready against the storm !
Riflemen, Riflemen, Riflemen form !

Form, be ready to do or die !
Form in Freedom's name and the Queen's !
True we have got—*such* a faithful ally
That only the Devil can tell what he means.
Form, Form, Riflemen Form !
Ready, be ready to meet the storm !
Riflemen, Riflemen, Riflemen form !

On 12 May a War Office circular approved the Volunteer movement. And by 18 May the Prince Consort could derive comfort from the fact that :

The people are demanding arms, and petitions come from every town for permission to form Volunteer Corps—not to help the French, but to guard against them ! Because popular instinct teaches the man in the street who his enemy is and of what the Italian war is merely the first Act.[1]

[1] To the Prince Regent of Prussia (ed. Jagow, *Letters of the Prince Consort*, p. 322). See C. Sebag-Montefiore, *A History of the Volunteer Forces* (London, 1908), ch. xii

Associated with this movement, strangely enough, was an agitation for neutrality, or ' non-intervention '. All this martial ardour was purely defensive. ' There is so much to repel the sympathies of a free country ', said the *Saturday Review*, ' in the conduct of all the belligerents, that for once, the voice of the country is absolutely unanimous in favour of neutrality.' Liberal hopes were expressed by *The Economist*, which believed that, if England stood aloof now, ' whenever the time for diplomatic negotiation [came] ', she would be able to advocate effectively ' the guaranteed independence of Italy of *every* foreign power '. Conservatives feared, with *The Times*, that in the end England might not be able to avoid fighting France.[1] But, whatever the shade of opinion, the recommended policy at the moment was the same. The *Leeds Express*, a Radical paper, violent for Italy, and rabid for Volunteers ; the *Leeds Intelligencer*, Conservative, and strong for treaties ; the Liberal and Nonconformist *Leeds Mercury* : all demanded neutrality.[2] Numerous meetings in favour of non-intervention were being held up and down the country. Napoleon III had commissioned Kossuth to campaign for neutrality in England, and he found considerable enthusiasm and wide agreement.[3] Malmesbury was hardly exaggerating when he informed Prussia that neutrality ' may be said to be the only [point] in which the English people appear to be at the present moment absorbed.' [4]

Opinion had shifted again. But the change was not great. England had not become wholeheartedly pro-Italian. Fear of France still weighed more heavily than feeling for Italy. She

[1] *Saturday Review*, 7 May. *The Economist*, 11 June. *The Times*, 25 May
[2] esp. *Leeds Express*, 7 May, 28 May ; *Leeds Intelligencer*, 30 April : *Leeds Mercury*, 24 May
[3] L. Kossuth, *Memories of My Exile* (London, 1880), ch. iii ; Urban, *British Opinion and Policy*, pp. 206–08
[4] 2 May (*Correspondence*, p. 377)

had, however, turned more completely isolationist. As Greville wrote :

The sentiments of people here are of a very mixed and almost contradictory character, for they are on the whole anti-Austrian, anti-French, and though more indulgent to the Sardinians than they deserve, not favourable to them. The most earnest and general desire is that we should keep out of the *mêlée*, and any termination of the war would be hailed with gladness, because we should thereby be relieved from our apprehensions of being involved in it. We should not be sorry to see the Austrians driven out of Italy for good and all, though most people would regret that the Emperor Louis Napoleon should be triumphant, and that such a course of perfidy, falsehood, and selfish ambition should be crowned with success.[1]

Monckton Milnes, a pro-Italian M.P. and supporter of Palmerston, was asked by French friends : ' What do you English really want ? ' ' We want,' he answered, ' first, that the Austrians should beat you French thoroughly ; next, we want that the Italians should be free ; and then we want them to be very grateful to us for doing nothing towards it.' [2] Various poets and writers—the Brownings, Ruskin, Arnold—castigated this selfish attitude. But they fully realised how few Englishmen agreed with them.[3]

III

By a remarkable chance, the outbreak of the Franco-Austrian War coincided with the beginning of the English

---

[1] 26 June (*The Greville Memoirs*, vol. viii, pp. 254–5)
[2] Quoted in ed. E. T. Cook & A. Wedderburn, *The Works of John Ruskin* (London, 1903–12), vol. xviii, p. xxiii
[3] Urban, *British Opinion and Policy*, pp. 209–10 ; ed. F. G. Kenyon, *Letters of E. B. Browning* (London, 1897), vol. ii, ch. x ; ed. Cook & Wedderburn, *Works of Ruskin*, vol. xviii, pp. 537–45 ; ed. M. M. Bevington, *Matthew Arnold's ' England and the Italian Question '* (Durham, N. Carolina, 1953)

General Election. The Conservative Government had been defeated in the House of Commons over Parliamentary Reform on 31 March. It took until 19 April to clear up outstanding business, and on 23 April the actual dissolution was proclaimed. Polling was spread out over a month, but the last returns were made before the end of May.[1]

For the purposes of this book, it is necessary to study the General Election only in order to determine how far the Italian Question affected it. Undoubtedly foreign policy received much attention during the campaign. At first, naturally, Reform had been regarded as the main issue. The coming Election had even been described as a plebiscite on the Conservatives' Reform Bill.[2] But the Government made no promise to reintroduce that measure or to propound a new scheme. In fact, ' sponging off his own Reform Bill from the British mind, Lord Derby wrote in its stead the question he wished to put to the nation,—What party would they have to reign over them ? ' So *The Times* on 11 May ; and it went on to claim that in any case the question of war had now ' almost overlaid ' that of Reform. This is disputable.[3] There was much discussion of Reform at the hustings, not only of past Conservative proposals but also of Liberal promises for the future. It is hardly possible to decide whether Reform or foreign policy counted for more. But at least it can safely be said that these two were the only topical issues of principle which could seriously have affected the Election.

Neither issue was clear-cut. The differences between the parties over Reform were small : both sides advocated some

[1] The principal source of my general account of the Election is *The Times*, supplemented by other newspapers and the remarks of contemporary statesmen.
[2] Martin, *Life of the Prince Consort*, vol. iv, p. 414
[3] See F. E. Gillespie, *Labor and Politics in England, 1850–67* (Durham, N. Carolina, 1927), chs. vi–vii

change, and the main question seemed to be, which side should do the deed ?[1] It soon emerged that much the same was true of the foreign-policy issue. Immediately after the Austrian ultimatum, indeed, Prince Albert was afraid that 'the affair may cost our ministry its elections, as it is sure to be regarded as responsible for the encouragement which has led Austria to take this violent step.'[2] And the Opposition leaders tried to take advantage of the false position in which the Government had placed itself in the debate of 18 April. Russell quickly issued a new election manifesto accusing the Conservatives of Austrian proclivities. Palmerston, hitherto so moderate, made a speech in his constituency at Tiverton attacking Austria's administration of Lombardy and her evil influence in the rest of Italy, and blaming the Government for not adhering to the French alliance.[3] The Economist menaced Ministers with ' a cry far louder than any Reform cry ', which would drive them from office. Some Radicals demanded greater sympathy for Italy.[4] But the Government, realising its error, hastened to correct it. Derby's public condemnation of Austria was so strongly worded that, to the Queen's delight, Russell dissented from it.[5] The extent of Ministers' concern is shown by the fact that Derby and Malmesbury battled continually with the Court in order to keep England's policy in line with public feeling. On 1 May the Prime Minister warned the Queen that ' no Government which could be formed in this country could hope to carry public opinion with it in taking an active part, as matters now stand in opposition to France and Russia.'[6]

[1] See A. Briggs, The Age of Improvement (London, 1959), p. 416
[2] 26 April, to King Leopold (Martin, Life of the Prince Consort, vol. iv, p. 430). cf. Malmesbury, Memoirs, p. 481
[3] S. Walpole, The Life of Lord John Russell (London, 1889), vol. ii, pp. 303–04. H. C. F. Bell, Lord Palmerston (London, 1936), vol. ii, pp. 209–10
[4] The Economist, 23 April. See Duncombe's speech in the debate of 18 April (Parl. Deb., 3rd series, vol. cliii, cols. 1879–81)
[5] 27 April, the Queen to Malmesbury (RA J. 18/124)
[6] QVL, vol. iii, p. 330

Two days later Malmesbury refused to insert in a dispatch some strictures on France, which the Queen had suggested adding, on the ground that ' the Govt. will have a very difficult task in laying these papers before Parliament, to avoid any appearance of partiality either for one side or the other.' [1] Later, when the Court was lamenting Austrian defeats, he told the Queen that ' this country would not go to war even in support of Italian independence, and there would not be ten men in the House of Commons who would do so on behalf of Austria.' [2] Derby had to use the same kind of arguments to preserve the right neutral tone in the Queen's Speech at the opening of the new Parliament.[3] The only royal success was the stopping of Malmesbury's telegram welcoming the Russian offer to assist England's efforts at localisation. Otherwise the Prime Minister and the Foreign Secretary had their way. Evidently the Government managed also to convey the desired impression to the electorate. Azeglio summarised the attitudes of the election candidates as follows :

I have observed that none of the orators has dared to back Austrian policy or to hazard the advice that England should tie herself to Austria's destinies. Some candidates have, on the other hand, had the courage to put forward ideas favourable to direct co-operation with Sardinia. All of them, however, including the Ministers, have unanimously advised the preservation of the most absolute neutrality.[4]

There was little dispute over present policy. The disagreement was about past history. It could be, and often was, argued that a more experienced or less prejudiced Foreign Secretary and Cabinet would have formed a juster appreciation of Austria's

---

[1] RA J. 19/17   [2] 29 May (Malmesbury, *Memoirs*, p. 488)
[3] See below
[4] 4 May, to Cavour (Archivio del Ministero degli Affari Esteri, Rome : Correspondence of the Sardinian Legation in London, Cartella lxxxviii)

intentions, and so perhaps would have been able to avert war. In future it would be better to trust to the Liberals.

The Government's defeat on 31 March had been by 39 votes in a House of 626, including the Speaker and tellers. (654 was then the full complement of M.P.s.) According to *The Times*, three ministerialists had voted with the Opposition, and 32 of the Opposition with the Government[1]—the Opposition had a *nominal* majority of about a hundred. At the Election the Conservatives gained—this too is *The Times'* figure —26 seats.[2] On a count by party allegiance, therefore, the Government was still in a minority by about fifty votes.

It was an exceptionally quiet Election, judged by the number of constituencies in which contests occurred : only 158, out of a possible 399.[3] Such contests as did take place do not seem to have been much affected by national issues. As *The Times* commented, this was normal :

An English borough of the genuine old stamp, with its 1,200 or 1,500 electors, is always prepared for a fight, but the rivalry, except in remarkable incidents, finds its aliment and its expression in the politics of the place itself. It is not that the constituency puts its own affairs above those of the nation, but that the national affairs do not penetrate, under ordinary circumstances, much below the surface of opinion. At periods, like that of 1832, there is a strong and decided set of the current, but at such periods only. In 1857 Lord Palmerston owed much to the popularity of the immediate question on which Parliament was dissolved, and probably the returns were really influenced by the national sentiment on the Chinese war. . . . But . . . the most severe and memorable contests, whether in counties or boroughs, have not been occasioned by the importance of the principles at stake, but by the wealth, emulation, and pugnacity of the competitors. A

---

[1] *The Times*, 2 April   [2] *The Times*, 24 May
[3] This figure is calculated from the lists in the *Annual Register*. For comparisons see N. Gash, *Politics in the Age of Peel* (London, 1953), p. 441 ; and H. J. Hanham, *Elections and Party Management* (London, 1959), p. 197.

really great question, indeed, rather diminishes strife by giving one party a preponderance too great to be cordially encountered.[1]

Greville recorded, moreover, on 17 May :

The general election has been eminently satisfactory in this, that it has elicited the completely Conservative spirit of the country. Palmerston, who predicted that the consequence would be a large increase of Radical strength, has been altogether mistaken. It may be added (whether this is a good or an evil) that it has also manifested the indifference of the country to all parties and to all political ties and connexions. In the last general election the cry was all for Palmerston, in this there has been no cry for anybody.[2]

The Conservatives' successes, *The Times* claimed, were simply :

about the number which a Government having the management of a Dissolution may calculate on gaining if the popular current does not run very vigorously either way, and if a wholesale and unscrupulous use is made of those elements of corruption which must, from the nature of things, be at the disposal of the Executive Government.[3]

Or earlier, considering the question from another angle :

The election of 1857 had been one of enormous and unprecedented gain to the Liberal party, . . . more nominal than real. . . . It could hardly be expected that so large a nominal gain could be retained, and any moderate loss—anything, for instance, not exceeding the loss of 20 seats—will be to the Liberal party a real and substantial victory.[4]

It is significant that the calculations of the two parties before the dissolution were reasonably accurate. Disraeli gathered from the Conservative agents that he could expect to win forty seats. ' Hayter', wrote Russell, ' says we shall only lose

[1] 19 April   [2] *The Greville Memoirs*, vol. viii, pp. 245–6
[3] 13 May   [4] 2 May

10 or 11 seats on balance.'[1] After the event, neither side was surprised. Malmesbury told Cowley that ' Our Elections are as usual less good than the agents' reports.' Russell said, ' If the boroughs surpassed our hopes, the counties have exceeded our fears.' [2] The agents' errors cancel out. There is little sign of any special intervention of public feeling.

Only in Ireland is there pretty clear evidence that the foreign-policy issue affected the result of the Election. The remnants of the ' independent' Irish party had given general support to the Conservative Government until the beginning of 1859. They had obtained a number of concessions to Irish interests, but they were not entirely satisfied. The question arose, whether they should continue to back the Administration. They could not agree, and in the division on the Reform Bill the party finally split : six voted for, and five against, the Bill. An important reason adduced for supporting the Conservatives was that their foreign policy was more acceptable to Roman Catholics than the Liberals'. Maguire, one of the six, wrote : ' To save Europe from the horrors of war, Italy from anarchy, and Rome from revolution, I voted against Lord John Russell, and the more dangerous incendiary, Lord Palmerston.' [3] The Roman Catholic interest, already divided, had now another ground of difference : Cardinal Wiseman of Westminster, with many Irish clergy, commended those who had voted with the Government ; Archbishop MacHale of Tuam took the opposite stand. Both groups of ' independent' M.P.s were returned at the Election. So nothing was decided by it. But it seems plain that the clerical split—widened by the foreign-policy

---

[1] *The Greville Memoirs*, vol. viii, p. 243 ; 26 April, Russell to Clarendon (Bodleian MS Clar. dep. c.104)

[2] 30 April (CP F.O. 519/196) ; 10 May, Russell to Parkes [not Parker, as Gooch says] (ed. Gooch, *Later Correspondence of Russell*, vol. ii, p. 230)

[3] Quoted in J. H. Whyte, *The Independent Irish Party 1850–9* (Oxford, 1958), p. 153

issue—played into the hands of the Conservatives over Ireland as a whole. The Chief Secretary for Ireland reckoned that the Ministry had won eight seats[1] ; and the General Election of 1859 marks the highest point of Conservative success in Ireland after the great Reform Act.[2]

As far as the General Election is concerned, then, it is impossible to uphold the view that England's Italian policy was the crucial issue in the political crisis of 1859. Still less can it be sustained that the Government lost many votes by its Austrian sympathies—an interpretation not uncommon in standard histories. Since the Conservatives *gained* seats, it would be more natural to contend, if their foreign policy had been an important issue, that the electorate *approved* that policy ; and the best-attested effect of the issue—in Ireland— would tend to support this argument. But in fact the issue was ill-defined, and was of small account in the Election.[3]

IV

Since the Election did not give the Conservatives a clear majority, it was left to the House of Commons—as usual during this period—to ' elect ' a Ministry. Again, for the purposes of this book, it is necessary to deal with the change of Government only in order to determine how far the Italian Question affected it.

[1] 17 May, Lord Naas to Disraeli (Buckle, *Disraeli*, vol. iv, p. 242)

[2] Whyte, *The Independent Irish Party*, p. 171. This paragraph is based on the account in Whyte's book of the last months of the independent party, esp. pp. 151–5 and pp. 165–74. cf. *The Times*, 21 May and *passim* ; and *The Greville Memoirs*, vol. viii, p. 246.

[3] I know of no full study of this Election. But there is a useful article by W. L. Guttsman, ' The General Election of 1859 in the Cities of Yorkshire ', *International Review of Social History*, vol. ii (1957), pp. 231–58. See also J. B. Conacher, ' Party Politics in the Age of Palmerston ', in ed. P. Appleman, W. A. Madden & M. Wolff, ' *1859* ' : *Entering an Age of Crisis* (Bloomington, 1959), pp. 163–80.

The House of Commons can rarely have been more anarchic than it was during the Derby Administration. The Peelite chiefs—Gladstone, Herbert, Sir James Graham, Edward Cardwell—were still isolated. The Irish were more divided than ever. Palmerston and Russell were rivals for the leadership of the Liberals. Indeed Sir George Lewis, a Palmerstonian who had been Chancellor of the Exchequer from 1855 to 1858, went so far as to declare, in September 1858 :

I consider the Liberal party at present to be extinct as a *party*. There is in the House of Commons a majority composed of persons holding Liberal opinions which no dissolution will, I believe, convert into a minority ; but the only organisation which at present exists within it is for the purpose of keeping in the Government and preventing the formation of a Liberal ministry.[1]

Lewis was referring to the fact that many Liberals of Russell's group, as well as many Radicals, were supporting Derby as Prime Minister rather than risk assisting the return of Palmerston. In the same month the Prince Consort wrote in a memorandum :

A House of Commons, having been elected solely for the object, and on the ground of supporting Lord Palmerston personally . . . holds him suddenly in such abhorrence, that not satisfied with having upset his Government, . . . it will hardly listen to him when he speaks. He is frequently received with hooting, and throughout the last session, it sufficed that [he] took up any cause for the whole House voting against it . . . merely to have the satisfaction of putting him into a minority.[2]

While Palmerston's prestige had fallen, Russell's had risen. But there seemed no hope of a reconciliation between them,

[1] To Henry Reeve : Ed. Sir G. F. Lewis, *Letters of Sir George Cornewall Lewis* (London, 1870), p. 344   [2] *QVL*, vol. iii, p. 300

although that alone would make possible a strong Liberal Government.

After the Election the position appeared at first sight even worse. The most coherent group in the House was the 300-odd Conservatives ; and the ' majority composed of persons holding Liberal opinions ' had been reduced. As Russell said : ' The mere distinction of " liberals " and " conservatives " does not at all tell how members will vote on a want of confidence motion.'[1] ' The Government ', wrote Herbert :

> will muster 300 men at least, who will run together like a pack of hounds ; add to these some half-dozen Irish Roman Catholics, who will always be glad to support them on a pinch, a few extreme Radicals . . ., and a few crotchety Liberals. . . . This brings members nearly to a tie, and at any rate does not constitute a very encouraging prospect on which to form a Government if a vote of censure be carried.

But the Election had had this gratifying result : it had revived party spirit among M.P.s, and altered the Opposition's attitude to the Government. There had previously been, continued Herbert :

> a kind of tacit understanding that the Parliament, which had tolerated the formation of a Government by a minority, was also to tolerate its continuance.
>
> Since that, the Government has set up for itself, has spurned the understanding, and defied the Liberal party. An acquiescence in their continued exercise of power would be an avowal of helpless disunion.[2]

There was a chance that, for once, if only Palmerston and Russell could come to an arrangement, nearly all the Liberals would vote together when Parliament met. There was also

[1] 10 May, Russell to Parkes (ed. Gooch, *Later Correspondence of Russell*, vol. ii, p. 230)

[2] 17 May, to Russell : Lord Stanmore, *Sidney Herbert : A Memoir* (London, 1906), vol. ii, pp. 182–4

a prospect that the remaining Peelites would all back a Liberal Ministry if one could be formed : Graham and Herbert definitely intended to do so, but Gladstone was still in doubt. The second rank of Opposition leaders—Lewis, Graham, Herbert and Lord Granville, the Liberal Leader in the House of Lords—set about planning the Conservatives' overthrow. Herbert wrote to Granville on 27 May :

> I am satisfied that if any step is taken to turn out the Government two things are necessary, viz. first, that the two rivals should agree to serve together as the Queen may direct. Secondly, to take the whole Liberal party into counsel, discuss the risks involved, and the objects to be attained. . . . The party require it and have a right to demand it. They are very independent . . ., and the time is gone by when they will vote like a flock of sheep for whatever some half-dozen men may concoct in a library. Depend upon it without previous frank conversation and interchange of opinion, no estimate can be formed of the chances of durability of a Liberal Government, and without such an estimate it is madness to turn out the existing Ministry.[1]

The procedure Herbert suggested was adopted, and had the desired result.

At every stage the foreign-policy issue received some attention. Herbert mentioned it during the early negotiations :

> As regards foreign affairs, there was a time when the Government could have used strong language against whoever should break the public peace, but now that it is broken there must be an honest neutrality. I agree with you [Russell] that the late antecedents of the Government make it almost impossible that their neutrality should be so looked upon.[2]

When making an overture to Palmerston, Russell said : ' The questions of reform, & foreign affairs require some previous

---

[1] Fitzmaurice, *Granville*, vol. i, p. 328
[2] 17 May (Stanmore, *Sidney Herbert*, vol. ii, pp. 183–4)

understanding, not as to details, but as to the Spirit in which they should be treated.'[1] Accordingly, on 20 May, the rivals 'talked over the four points : 1 Foreign Affairs. 2 Reform. 3 Amendment on Address. 4 Composition of any Government that might succeed to the present.'[2] There were four possible issues on which the Conservatives might have been brought down : the 'criminality' of the dissolution, foreign affairs, Reform, and simple want of confidence.[3] It was decided to propose to the party meeting that the last be chosen. This was Herbert's report of the proceedings, in Willis's Rooms on 6 June :

There were about 280 members present, which is thought very large, as the Irish members are not yet come over in any number. . . . Pam. spoke shortly and well, described the challenge in the Queen's dissolution speech, alluded to the failures of the Government in legislation, and the danger of their involving us in a war, said that he and Johnny were at one (great cheering). Then there was a pause, and a call for Lord John, who spoke in the same sense, and said if the vote succeeded it was necessary to look forward, and if the Queen sent for Pam., he, Johnny, would cheerfully co-operate with him in the formation of a Government—broad basis, etc.—and then Pam. whispered to him, and he added as much for Pam. Then calls for Bright, who spoke in a—for him—decent manner enough ; said the differences had been in the party as well as the leaders, and the fault of the leaders. Wanted some clearer assurance about war, but upon the whole promised co-operation. Pam. gave the clearer assurance, and I got up. . . . I preached union, and said I did not mind if we were beat, as if we are a minority we should know our place and watch, but also support the Government in all national matters. Then came Mr. E. James, Mr. Loch, Mr. Monckton Milnes, Mr. Roebuck, Mr. Horsman, Mr. Lindsay,

[1] 18 May (BMS)
[2] 21 May, Russell to Herbert (Stanmore, *Sidney Herbert*, vol. ii, pp. 186–7)
[3] 16 May, the same to the same (*ibid.* vol. ii, pp. 181–2) ; 27 May, Granville to Herbert (Fitzmaurice, *Granville*, vol. i, p. 330)

Mr. Ellice, Col. Dearing. The underlined men *against*. Roebuck very ill received, Horsman only raising difficulties, and wanting it put off for ten days, but the rest all for. So the proposition was put and carried amidst loud cheers, and Lord Hartington and Mr. Hanbury are to move and second the identical amendment which Peel carried against Lord Melbourne in 1841. On the whole it was very successful, no one objecting who was not expected to do so, and others concurring who had not been reckoned on.[1]

One further vital piece of information about the meeting can be culled from the account in *The Times* : Palmerston had again emphasised the need to revive the French alliance. ' No consideration', concluded a leader-writer, ' seems to have weighed more on the mind of the meeting . . . than the obvious inability of our Foreign Minister to give effect to his propositions or remonstrances.' [2]

In preparation for the great Commons debate, Derby, arguing with the Queen about the wording of her Speech at the opening of Parliament, had done his best to safeguard the Ministry from the most probable accusations against its foreign policy :

As matters stand at present, Lord Derby is warranted in assuring your Majesty that if there is one subject on which more than another the mind of the country is unanimous, it is that of an entire abstinence from participation in the struggle now going on in Italy. He collects this from the language of politicians of almost every class, from all the public papers, from Addresses and Memorials which he receives every day—some urging, and some congratulating him upon the adoption of a perfectly neutral policy. The sympathies of the country are neither with France nor with Austria, but were it not for the intervention of France, they would be general in favour of Italy. The charge now made against

[1] To Mrs Herbert (Stanmore, *Sidney Herbert*, vol. ii, pp. 198–9)
[2] 7 June. cf. *The Greville Memoirs*, vol. viii, p. 251

your Majesty's servants, by the opposition Press, as the *Morning Post* and *Daily News*, is that their neutrality covers such wishes and designs in favour of Austria ; and any word in your Majesty's Speech which should imply a doubt of the continuance of strict impartiality, would, undoubtedly, provoke a hostile Amendment, which might very possibly be carried in the Sardinian sense. . . . There is, at this moment, in the country, a great jealousy and suspicion of France, . . . but it is neutralised, partly by sympathy for Italy, partly by suspicions, industriously circulated, of the pro-Austrian tendencies of the present Government. It is very important that the language of the Speech should be so decided as to negative this impression. . . . If there be no attempt made to run counter to public opinion, and Austria should sustain serious reverses, the jealousy of France will increase, and the feeling of the country will support your Majesty in a war, should such arise, against her aggression ; but if the slightest pretext be afforded for doubting the *bonâ fide* character of British neutrality, or the firm determination to maintain it, an anti-German feeling will be excited, which will be fatal to the Administration, and seriously embarrassing to your Majesty.[1]

Despite Derby's efforts, there was a good deal of suspicion expressed in the debate, which occupied the nights of 7, 9 and 10 June. Much of the discussion turned on foreign affairs. The Government was inclined to appeal to Malmesbury's record as an impartial, peaceable and reliable Foreign Secretary for its justification. It had had, after all, little success in domestic matters, and had made no promises to be active at home in the future. The Opposition naturally retorted that Malmesbury had not in fact averted war, that the Government had not always appeared to be entirely impartial, and that it had hinted at the possibility of England's having to take part in the war. Several of the speakers in the debate specifically referred to the foreign-policy issue as predominant.[2]

[1] 2 June (*QVL*, vol. iii, pp. 337-8). cf. Buckle, *Disraeli*, vol. iv, pp. 245-6
[2] *Parl. Deb.*, 3rd series, vol. cliv, cols. 146, 205-6, 249, etc.

By 323 votes to 310, in a very full House indeed, the Government was defeated, and it at once resigned. Of English Liberals, Lindsay and Roebuck were the most important of the handful—estimates vary from six to ten—who voted with the Conservatives. Both of them criticised the attitude of Palmerston on foreign policy as well as on Reform.[1] Of Irish Liberals, between seven and eleven voted for Derby, including five of the six 'independents' who had supported his Reform Bill. Of reputed Conservatives, no more than one or two opposed the Government. Gladstone voted Conservative; Horsman voted Liberal.[2] Gladstone made no speech; Horsman explained that he found great difficulty in reaching a decision, and wished that Malmesbury's Blue Book had been made available to assist him.[3]

To establish that the foreign-policy issue was of crucial importance in bringing about the fall of the Government, it would presumably be necessary to show that, if Liberals had not disapproved of Malmesbury's attitude in the international crisis, the Conservatives would have been able to maintain themselves in office. It could never be easy to prove —or disprove—such a proposition; and in this case the evidence is by no means conclusive. But the probabilities are that the proposition is false.

The original Government defeat in the House of Commons was over Reform, and the dissolution followed from that. Given a dissolution and an election campaign, it seems practically certain that, whatever foreign policy the Ministry had

[1] ibid., vol. cliv, cols. 311–16 and 390–5
[2] The figures of non-party voting are derived from *The Times* of 13 June, the *Daily News* of 13 June, and from a comparison between the party-affiliations attributed to Members in *Dod's Parliamentary Companion* for 1859 and the division list. Dod has a peculiar category of 65 Liberal-Conservatives, most of whom seem in fact to have been regular supporters of Derby; eight of them, however, including Cardwell and Herbert, voted Liberal. See also Whyte, *Independent Irish Party*, Appendix C; and Urban, *British Opinion and Policy*, p. 229n.   [3] *Parl. Deb.*, 3rd series, vol. cliv, cols. 246–51

been pursuing, the Liberal sections would have reunited and then attempted to gain power. This, after all, is how the game of politics is played. The Liberal leaders deliberately chose to move a general motion of no-confidence rather than to censure any individual aspect of the Conservatives' record, largely because they were convinced that the general motion would receive the greatest support.[1] The critical division, therefore, purported to be a simple party vote ; and there is every reason to suppose that most Members regarded it in that light.

Nevertheless, it is conceivable that the foreign-policy issue was decisive in this sense : that it ensured the victory of the Opposition by determining seven or more wavering Liberals to vote with their party. The margin is so small that an issue of much less significance than that of Malmesbury's foreign policy might plausibly be held to have been a crucial factor. There is no direct evidence that any Liberal grounded his support of the no-confidence motion on his objections to the Government's foreign policy alone. But Conservatives did contend after the debate that, if the Blue Book had been available before the division, the verdict would have been reversed. Malmesbury himself wrote :

> With a dead majority against him, it is evident that he [Derby] could not for long have maintained his ground, but it is equally certain that he would not have been defeated on the Address if Disraeli had previously laid on the table the Blue-Book containing the Italian and French correspondence with the Foreign Office. Why he chose not to do so I never knew . . . ; but . . . at least twelve or fourteen members of Parliament who voted against us in the fatal division came out of their way at different times and places to assure me that, had they read that correspondence before the debate, they never would have voted for an amendment which,

[1] 27 May, Granville to Palmerston (Fitzmaurice, *Granville*, vol. i, p. 330). cf. E. I. Barrington, *The Servant of All* (London, 1927), vol. i, p. 159

as far as our conduct respecting the War was concerned, was thoroughly undeserved. . . . Mr. Cobden was one of these.[1]

This statement was evidently written long after the event, and is not very convincing. It was most inept of Malmesbury to single out Cobden, who in fact took no part in the division, since he was in America.[2] But others made Malmesbury's point at the time. Lord Elcho, speaking in the House of Commons on 15 July, alleged that the production of the Blue Book would have made a difference of twenty votes.[3] When challenged in the debate of 8 August, however, he declined to give even one name ; the Members who then attacked Palmerston's Government had all, with the exception of Horsman, voted for Derby in the great division [4] ; and, to match Horsman, there is Gladstone, who would have voted against Derby instead of for him if he had been able to read the Blue Book first.[5] Even so, since the views of the great bulk of Members are unascertainable, it is not possible to refute completely Malmesbury's claim that, in this very limited sense, the foreign-policy issue was decisive. But the evidence in its favour is not impressive.

Foreign affairs were in everybody's mind. But the true significance of this episode is that, for once during this period, it was party solidarity, not individuals' feelings on a particular issue, which brought down a Government. In this respect the vote of 1859 differed markedly from those of 1855, 1857 and 1866. In 1859 such disagreement as existed over foreign policy ran on party lines.[6]

[1] Malmesbury, *Memoirs*, p. 491   [2] Morley, *Cobden*, p. 692
[3] *Parl. Deb.*, 3rd series, vol. cliv, col. 1304
[4] *ibid.* vol. clv, col. 1150 and cols. 1188–98
[5] This must be the meaning of Gladstone's remark in the debate of 8 August, *ibid.* vol. clv, col. 1150. cf. Lacaita, *An Italian Englishman*, p. 126.
[6] On the whole question of the Liberal consolidation and the vote of no-confidence, see : Stanmore, *Sidney Herbert*, vol. ii, pp. 181–99 ; Parker, *Graham*, vol. ii, pp. 381–8 ; Fitzmaurice, *Granville*, vol. i, pp. 327–31 ;

V

When the Conservative Government resigned, it was expected that Palmerston would be summoned by the Queen to form a new Administration. He was more generally acceptable as Prime Minister than Russell.[1] Instead, Granville was sent for. The Queen justified this step on the ground that, whereas there was no unchallenged Liberal leader in the House of Commons, Granville was universally acknowledged as leader in the House of Lords. In fact she must have known of the compact between Palmerston and Russell, and it is clear that she wished to avoid appointing either, chiefly because of her distrust of their views on foreign policy. Royal preoccupation with the war is very plain in the last weeks of the Derby Ministry; the Queen referred, in talking to Granville, to ' the effect likely to be produced on the Continent by Lord Palmerston's name, if he had the direction of Foreign Affairs '; and Prince Albert spoke of ' our attempt to get Granville with Clarendon at the Foreign Office '.[2] But, not surprisingly, though both Palmerston and Russell would agree to serve in second place, there seemed little prospect of obtaining the support of either as the third person in a Cabinet. Granville had to give up the task, and the Queen then sent for Palmerston.[3]

[1] See esp. 27 May, Herbert to Granville (Stanmore, *Sidney Herbert*, vol. ii, p. 194), and 28 May, Herbert to Gladstone (*ibid*. vol. ii, p. 195)
[2] *QVL*, vol. iii, p. 344. ed. Jagow, *Letters of the Prince Consort*, p. 336. ' Erhalten ' I have translated as ' get ' rather than ' have '.
[3] *The Greville Memoirs*, vol. viii, pp. 252–3 and 255–6. *QVL*, vol. iii, pp. 344–5. Fitzmaurice, *Granville*, vol. i, pp. 332–44

Walpole, *Russell*, vol. ii, pp. 304–06 ; Bell, *Palmerston*, vol. ii, pp. 212–14 ; ed. R. A. J. Walling, *The Diaries of John Bright* (London, 1930), pp. 237–40 ; Buckle, *Disraeli*, vol. iv, pp. 235–53 and 259–60 ; Morley, *Gladstone*, vol. i, pp. 621–5 ; *The Greville Memoirs*, vol. viii, pp. 245–51.

Russell insisted on the Foreign Office : ' The importance of European affairs at the moment is my temptation and justification.'[1] Clarendon declined to serve in any other position. Graham had already announced that he would take no part. Gladstone insisted on the Exchequer. Lewis, who had just accepted that post again, had to give way, and was relegated to the Home Office. Granville received the Presidency of the Council. Cobden was offered the Board of Trade. The rest of the Cabinet consisted of four Palmerstonians, three Peelites and another Radical, with a compromise Lord Chancellor, Lord Campbell, and with a supporter of Russell, the Duke of Somerset, as First Lord of the Admiralty. Of the Palmerstonians, the Duke of Argyll became Lord Privy Seal, Lord Elgin Postmaster-General, Sir Charles Wood Secretary for India, and Sir George Grey Chancellor of the Duchy. The Duke of Newcastle was given the Secretaryship for the Colonies, Herbert the War Office, and Cardwell the Irish Secretaryship—the three Peelites. Milner Gibson was made President of the Poor Law Board—the Radical office *par excellence*. When, on his return from America, Cobden refused to serve, Gibson moved to the Board of Trade, and C. P. Villiers (brother of Clarendon and brother-in-law of Lewis), who had once been a prominent figure in the Free Trade agitation but was a dowdy Radical now, took the Poor Law Board.[2] In this way the Peelites were absorbed into the reunited Liberal party.

Gladstone's acceptance of the Exchequer was remarkable in view of his vote for Derby in the no-confidence debate. Five years later he explained his action as follows :

[1] Walpole, *Russell*, vol. ii, p. 309n

[2] Bell, *Palmerston*, vol. ii, pp. 216–19 ; Fitzmaurice, *Granville*, vol. i, pp. 344–6 ; Stanmore, *Sidney Herbert*, vol. ii, pp. 199–201 ; Sir H. E. Maxwell, *The Life and Letters of the Fourth Earl of Clarendon* (London, 1913), vol. ii, pp. 185–8 ; Morley, *Cobden*, pp. 690–8

When I took my present office in 1859, I had several negative and several positive reasons for accepting it. Of the first, there were these. There had been differences and collisions, but there were no resentments. I felt myself to be mischievous in an isolated position, outside the regular party organization of Parliament. And I was aware of no difference of opinion or tendency likely to disturb the new government. Then on the positive side. I felt sure that in finance there was still much useful work to be done. I was desirous to co-operate in settling the question of the franchise, and failed to anticipate the disaster that it was to undergo. My friends were enlisted, or I knew would enlist. . . . And the overwhelming interest and weight of the Italian question, and of our foreign policy in connection with it, joined to my entire mistrust of the former government in relation to it, led me to decide without one moment's hesitation.[1]

This has the flavour of self-justification : Gladstone often wondered whether he had been wise to join a Government, many of whose policies he was to find disagreeable ; and he looked on his efforts to ' assist its Italian purposes ' as a principal count in his vindication. But he had, on 9 July 1859, written to Massari, one of Cavour's most intimate associates :

I can assure you that among the very first and foremost motives which have guided me in returning to office under the Crown, perhaps I should go further and say the very first of them all, has been a consideration of the great Italian question in its present state, and of the important though I hope pacific part which England may have to play in bringing it to a happy settlement.[2]

Some of the other motives, however, were very powerful. His position was difficult, and his attitude complex. He had abandoned the Conservatives with Peel, and then in 1855 he had left Palmerston. In the following years he established

[1] To Acton (Morley, *Gladstone*, vol. i, p. 628)
[2] GP BM Add MS 44530, f.47

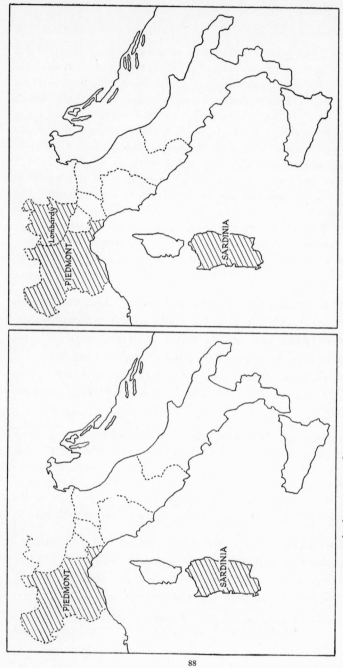

At the beginning of 1859

After July 1859

The unification of Italy, or the expansion of Piedmont-Sardinia

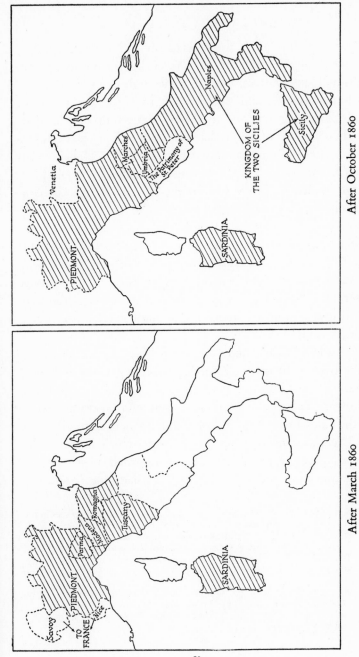

After March 1860

After October 1860

The unification of Italy, or the expansion of Piedmont-Sardinia

himself as Palmerston's most persistent and violent enemy.[1]
During the Derby Ministry of 1858-9 he voted consistently
with the Conservatives, went as their High Commissioner to
the Ionian Islands, and was thought to be on the point of
finally accepting office from them.[2] Yet, although he was
acutely conscious of his 'isolated position', he in fact refused
several offers of important posts in Derby's Cabinet, even
when accompanied by Disraeli's assurance that he would give
up the Leadership of the Commons, and even when Graham
counselled acceptance. He did not wish to join the Conservatives by himself; he believed that, without more substantial reinforcements, they would remain 'a constant
minority'; and he disliked Disraeli.[3] What he hoped was
that he would have the opportunity to take part in a strong
government when one could be formed, and to carry through
his great programme of reductions in indirect and, ultimately,
in direct taxation.[4]

He told Aberdeen and Graham in May 1858 that 'a man
at the bottom of the well must not try to get out, however
disagreeable his position, until a rope or a ladder is put down
to him.'[5] Palmerston's readiness, even after Gladstone's vote
for the Conservatives in the no-confidence debate, to give him
the Exchequer in a strong government which included the
remaining active Peelites, might be regarded as the perfect
rescue apparatus. But it may be that Gladstone would not

[1] Not only by his speeches in Parliament, but also by several articles in the
Quarterly Review : 'Prospects Political and Financial', vol. ci (1857),
pp. 243-84 ; 'The New Parliament and its Work', vol. ci (1857), pp. 541-
84 ; 'France and the Late Ministry', vol. ciii (1858), pp. 526-74 ; and
'The Past and Present Administrations', vol. civ (1858), pp. 515-60.
[2] Stanmore, *Sidney Herbert*, vol. ii, p. 197. Morley, *Gladstone*, vol. i,
pp. 594-620
[3] Parker, *Graham*, vol. ii, pp. 345-53. Buckle, *Disraeli*, vol. iv, pp. 157-9,
241. Morley, *Gladstone*, vol. i, pp. 551-6, 558-67, 576-91
[4] Parker, *Graham*, vol. ii, pp. 298-9 ; Morley, *Gladstone*, vol. i, pp. 552-3
[5] *ibid.* vol. i, p. 585

have availed himself even of this alluring means of escape if he had not also found a question of principle on which he agreed with his would-be rescuer. This is the importance of the foreign-policy issue in Gladstone's case. Before he passed through Italy in March 1859 he had been particularly bitter against Palmerston's foreign policy, and particularly appreciative of Malmesbury's.[1] He reached England, as he had from Naples in 1851, enthusiastic for the Italian cause and sympathetic with Palmerston's views. According to Aberdeen, ' The most brilliant stroke made was Palmerston's speech at Tiverton. His declared wish to see the Austrians turned out of Italy by the war has secured Gladstone.' [2] If there had been no Italian crisis and Gladstone had still received the same offer from Palmerston, it is quite impossible to guess what he would have done. No more can be said than that, as things happened, the Italian crisis and the foreign-policy issue made it easier for him to join Palmerston.[3]

VI

From the Cavourians' point of view, the vote of the House of Commons was a great victory, and the Piedmontese and French representatives cheered it indecorously from the lobby.[4] The Prince Consort lamented that :

[1] See Q.R., vol. civ (1858), p. 517 etc.
[2] Parker, Graham, vol. ii, p. 388
[3] Morley, Gladstone, vol. i, pp. 627-33. cf. P. Magnus, Gladstone (London, 1954), pp. 139-40
I was fortunate to be able to read, through the kindness of Professor Asa Briggs, an unpublished Gladstone Prize (Oxford University) essay by G. H. L. Le May, ' Mr Gladstone and Italy, to 1874 '; and, through the kindness of Professor R. F. Treharne, a typescript article by S. Gopal, ' Gladstone and the Italian Question ', since published in History, vol. xli (1956), pp. 113-21.
[4] Malmesbury, Memoirs, p. 490. ed. L. Fagan, Lettere ad A. Panizzi (Florence, 1880), p. 324

We have got a Ministry which exactly suits Louis Napoleon. . . .

Palmerston is anti-Austrian, pro-Italian, and especially pro-Napoleon ; Lord John is anti-French, but strongly pro-Italian ; Sidney Herbert, Granville, the Duke of Newcastle, Sir George Cornewall Lewis, and Lord Elgin are anti-French and on the whole pro-Austrian ; Gladstone is violently pro-Italian. Sir George Grey, Sir Charles Wood, Mr. Cardwell, and the Duke of Argyll are quite neutral. Mr. Milner Gibson admires Mazzini and Kossuth and was a bosom friend of Orsini . . . ![1]

This outcome cannot, however, be considered a triumph of the electorate or of Parliament over the Conservatives' pro-Austrian policy. Before the Election, it is true, Aberdeen had believed ' the danger is great that the cause of Italian independence will be identified with Reform of Parliament, and a revolutionary character will thus be given to the struggle both at home and abroad.' [2] But in fact the popular reactions to the war were a demand for neutrality and a strong expression of opinion against France ; and foreign affairs attracted interest away from Reform. It was by an accident of Parliamentary politics, not by a deliberate verdict on foreign policy, that the pro-Italian triumvirate—Palmerston, Russell and Gladstone—was placed at the head of affairs.

[1] 15 June, to the Prince Regent of Prussia (ed. Jagow, *Letters of the Prince Consort*, p. 336) [2] 2 April (Parker, *Graham*, vol. ii, p. 376)

Chapter V

Villafranca, the Battle of the Peace and the Rise of the French Alliance

June 1859 to January 1860

PALMERSTON's Government, since it had a party majority in the House of Commons behind it, was much more powerful than Derby's. But the new Cabinet—partly because it contained the representatives of so many sections, but largely because of the personalities of the individual Ministers—was much less harmonious than the old. Within three weeks of the Administration's entering upon office, Russell's conduct of foreign policy had become the subject of bitter contention in the Cabinet.

The disputes are very well documented, especially those of December 1859–January 1860 ; and they are as interesting and significant as the developing policy which emerged from them. In this and the next Chapter a chronological account will be given of both. First, for clarity's sake, the attitudes of the principal contestants at the outset of the struggle, and the general nature of the disputes, will be outlined.

I

Palmerston himself had long been convinced that Austria should be removed from Italy.

As for myself [he wrote to Granville in January 1859], I am very Austrian north of the Alps, but very anti-Austrian south of the Alps. The Austrians . . . govern their own provinces ill, and are the props and encouragers of bad government in all the other states of the Peninsula, except in Piedmont, where fortunately they have no influence. . . .

I should therefore rejoice and feel relieved if Italy up to the Tyrol were freed from Austrian domination and military occupation.[1]

He had opposed a war provoked by France against Austria, because he feared the total destruction of the latter, whose existence as a Great Power he regarded as a vital English and European interest. But, after the Austrian ultimatum, the folly of which found him incredulous, he was pleased enough at the outbreak of war, expected France to make a quick victory, and rejoiced at the probability that Italy would soon be freed from Austrian rule.[2] He thought that English interests would be well served by the establishment in North Italy of a strong new state as a counterpoise both to France and Austria ; and he favoured the immediate annexation to Piedmont of the territories conquered by Napoleon.[3] His attitude had an idealistic—or at least an ideological—element in it : he was in no doubt that constitutional government would benefit any civilised state.[4] But he also had a quite exceptionally firm grasp of the realities of the Italian and European situation. He knew France was stronger than Austria and would defeat her ; he knew that only Piedmont among Italian states could fill Austria's place ; he knew that to strengthen Piedmont was the only means of reducing the

[1] Fitzmaurice, *Granville*, vol. i, pp. 325-6
[2] 24 April, to Clarendon (Maxwell, *Clarendon*, vol. ii, p. 184) ; 8 May, to Cowley (Wellesley, *The Paris Embassy*, pp. 181-2)
[3] Cabinet Memorandum of 28 June (RP PRO 30/22/27)
[4] See Sir C. Webster, *The Foreign Policy of Palmerston, 1830-41* (London, 1951), esp. vol. i, p. i, and vol. ii, ch. ix

influence which France would obtain in Italy by her victories ; and even his trust in the genuineness of Napoleon's Italian sympathies was well founded.

Russell had a much less practical approach to the problem. He judged the affairs of Italy by the far-fetched analogy of the Glorious Revolution : Cavour represented for him the Italian branch of Whiggery.[1] 'Tuscany', he thought, 'has made a good beginning, and in fact has a better case against Leopold 2nd for violating fundamental laws and withdrawing than we had against James 2nd.'[2] His constitutionalism was absurdly doctrinaire. He wished to revive the abortive Sicilian constitution of 1812, which he described as 'exactly our own, with the improvement that none of the taxes were to be exacted for more than one year'.[3] He was realistic in the sense that he did not ignore the factor of power, but not in the sense that his assessments of the situation were just. He claimed that, whereas Malmesbury had 'proposed to interfere on the side which was most in the right', 'I only propose to interfere where our own interests or honour shall require it.'[4] He spoke sometimes of 'that mechanical contrivance, the balance of power'.[5] But he was convinced that it was strategically vital to England that Austria should retain Venetia.[6] And he had close associations with Tuscan Liberals, many of whom were Tuscan rather than Italian patriots ; which no doubt partly accounts for the fact that, even in the full flush of French success, he wanted 'a power (sovereign or half-sovereign) interposed between Austria & the K. of Sardinia. I have no wish to see Piedmont stretch as far as

[1] 11 November 1858, to the Dean of Bristol (RP PRO 30/22/13)
[2] 19 May 1859, to Parkes (ed. Gooch, *Later Correspondence of Russell*, vol. ii, p. 230)   [3] 28 May 1860, to Palmerston (BMS)
[4] 28 June 1859, to Granville (Granville MSS. PRO 30/29/24)
[5] e.g. 25 August, to Corbett (Minister in Florence) (ed. Gooch, *Later Correspondence of Russell*, vol. ii, p. 238)
[6] 26 December 1858, to Clarendon (*ibid.* vol. ii, pp. 228-9)

Venice.'[1] Altogether, he was much less pro-French and pro-Piedmontese than Palmerston.

Despite these differences of opinion, the Prime Minister and Foreign Secretary usually acted together. Gladstone generally backed them, making 'a formidable phalanx' in Cabinet.[2] But his views were different again. He was obsessed with the problem of the Papacy. As for the aggrandisement of Piedmont, he retained his pre-war doubts, although he recognised that 'a kingdom of North Italy stretching from sea to sea' would not harm English interests. Writing at the end of June, he said :

> After the manner in which Austria has committed herself by crossing the Ticino Sardinia will doubtless look for some extension of territory. For one I cannot wish it to be large : partly for reasons stated above [Austrian enmity] : partly because after the experience of 1848-9 we cannot rely on the recent manifestation in Lombardy of a desire for annexation ; while the Papers appear to shew that in Tuscany *even* under present circumstances there has been much difference of opinion : partly because it seems uncertain how far Sardinia has mixed sheer ambition with those Italian aims which (I cannot but think) the absolute necessities of her position required her to adopt.

What he really hoped for was the establishment of a North Italian Kingdom independent of Austria but friendly to her ; and he suggested that Archduke Maximilian, who had already once attempted to liberalise Austrian rule in Italy, should be its ruler.[3] Like Russell, he was less pro-French than the Prime Minister at this stage.

Not infrequently, the triumvirate was to find itself opposed by the whole, or nearly the whole, of the rest of the Cabinet.

---

[1] Walpole, *Russell*, vol. ii, pp. 276-8 ; 28 June 1859, to Cowley (CP F.O. 519/197)　　[2] Fitzmaurice, *Granville*, vol. i, p. 346
[3] Cabinet Memorandum of 30 June (in RP PRO 30/22/19 and GP BM Add MS 44748, f.93ff.)

This was not because the remaining Ministers held views on the Italian Question as definite as, but different from, those of the three Italophiles. Most of them were without views on the matter. The argument was seldom about the aims of English foreign policy in Italy. Nominally at least, it was about means and methods. This was the normal division of opinion in the early months, as defined by Granville, the chief spokesman of the Cabinet majority :

Three or four of the Cabinet hold with Lord John that neutrality need not necessarily be accompanied by impartiality ; and that while we remain materially neutral, we may give our best wishes and the expression of those good wishes in favour of either party. The rest of the Cabinet are strongly of opinion, as far as I can gather (many of them being silent), that we ought to abstain from any demonstration on one side or the other, and that we ought to bide our time till we can really be of use ; but that when we are invited, or feel compelled by circumstances to come forward, we are then at liberty to propose what may appear to be the best settlement of affairs which *could* possibly be agreed to, without considering whether such settlement is more favourable or not to one party.[1]

Palmerston and Russell, and to a lesser extent Gladstone, seemed to be ready to state a view on the foreign situation at every opportunity, and to give counsel, warnings and recommendations to other Powers, without accepting responsibility for the consequences of following the advice. The remaining Ministers were reluctant to commit England to proposals which she might not have the power—and which they themselves had little desire—to enforce.

It was, however, somewhat doubtful constitutionally—and very doubtful in practice, if only because of the time factor—how far the Foreign Secretary should be expected to consult his

[1] 13 July, to the Prince Consort (Fitzmaurice, *Granville*, vol. i, p. 351)

fellow-Ministers. Although it was clearly for the Cabinet to prescribe the general lines of foreign policy, it was for him to carry out the agreed policy in detail. Usage, as laid down when Palmerston was dismissed in 1851, did not require the Foreign Secretary, in the ordinary way, to consult anyone save the Prime Minister and the Queen. It was left to the Prime Minister to ensure that the Cabinet's wishes were respected.[1] With Palmerston as Prime Minister this was an inadequate safeguard. Even before it was imagined that Russell might take the Foreign Office, Granville was ' most anxious that', if a Liberal Government were installed, ' a distinct pledge should be given that the Cabinet should be kept informed of everything that was done ' in foreign policy.[2] And Newcastle exacted such a pledge from Palmerston when he accepted office.[3] Russell acquiesced, but with an ominous qualification. ' I am quite ready', he wrote gaily to Palmerston, ' to confirm what you said to the D. of Newcastle. I should however rather try to imitate yr. practice when Foreign Minr. than Clarendon's.' [4] This is precisely what Russell attempted to do, with Palmerston's connivance, and to the indignation of the rest of the Cabinet.

In these circumstances the role of the Queen and the Prince Consort was vital. Although, as has been seen, they were firm believers in the merits of constitutional government, they considered that, as far as English interests were concerned, the political organisation of Italy before the outbreak of war was more satisfactory than any rearrangement made under French auspices was likely to be. They therefore tried to stop any expression of opinion, let alone action, by

---

[1] The main documents are in ed. G. M. Young and W. D. Handcock, *English Historical Documents, 1833–74* (London, 1956), pp. 70–80.
[2] 23 May 1859, to Herbert (Stanmore, *Sidney Herbert*, vol. ii, p. 188)
[3] J. Martineau, *The Life of . . . Newcastle* (London, 1908), pp. 285–6
[4] 16 June (PRO 30/22/13)

the 'Italian' Ministers. The Queen took full advantage of her undoubted right to be consulted before dispatches were sent in her name : she relentlessly criticised Russell's drafts, and she insisted that the Cabinet be summoned to discuss any points of principle that were raised. The Prince exploited his peculiar position in order to marshal the Cabinet majority against Palmerston and Russell. Though he was the Queen's principal adviser and confidant, he was not constitutionally 'responsible' ; and, though he claimed the deference due to royalty, he deigned to correspond with Ministers as a private person. At least five Ministers were prepared to report to him, or to his Private Secretary, the details of Cabinet discussions—Granville, Wood, Grey, Newcastle and Lewis ; and Clarendon, who, though not a Minister, was in the confidence of Palmerston, Lewis and Villiers, was equally complaisant.[1] It was through the efforts of the Queen and the Prince that the opposition to the triumvirate was enabled to exert a steady influence on foreign policy.

II

A dispatch to Bloomfield in Berlin, in which Russell abandoned the Conservative Government's attempt to uphold the *status quo ante bellum*, provoked the first serious clash. Among the Foreign Secretary's earliest productions, on 22 June, had been a reiteration of Malmesbury's advice to Prussia to remain neutral. The more radical document, of 7 July, effectively scotched a proposal from Berlin that the two Powers should at once mediate on the basis of the pre-

[1] Of Granville's many letters, not a few have been printed in QVL and Fitzmaurice's *Life*. Wood wrote the next largest number, addressed to General Grey, the Prince's Secretary. Sir George Grey is mentioned as giving information in RA J. 24/19, and Newcastle and Lewis in J. 23/135, both memoranda by the Prince.

war position. That was impracticable, said Russell : Austria must expect to surrender territory. In fact :

> Be their divisions and boundaries arranged as they may, it is the firm persuasion of Her Majesty's Government that an Italy in which the people should be 'free citizens of a great country' would strengthen and confirm the balance of power. . . .
>
> I must not omit to state that any settlement of Italy would, in the eyes of Her Majesty's Government, be incomplete, which did not effect a permanent reform in the administration of the States of the Church.
>
> Every one knows that Rome and the Legations have been much worse governed by the Pope's Ministers than Lombardy by Austrian Archdukes, and that would be a partial and unsatisfactory arrangement which struck down the rule of the latter, and left the former in all its deformity.[1]

Although such undiplomatic language enlivened the dispatch, it had been subjected to royal and Cabinet alterations. But the Court still had cause of complaint : it had not been re-submitted to the Queen after the Cabinet had modified it. This lapse, among others, caused the Prince to ask information from Granville, who replied that 'The Prussian despatch was sent in a form which was certainly not in accordance with the wishes of the Cabinet.' The Prime Minister and Foreign Secretary had foiled their colleagues on this occasion.[2]

French attempts to gain English approval for two sets of peace terms were the next cause of anxiety. The Cabinet decided to communicate the first set to Austria without comment, but Russell privately showed that he supported them. Both he and Palmerston wished to give 'moral support' to the second set. But the Queen and the Cabinet prevented it,

[1] *Prussia (Neutrality) : Copy of a Despatch . . . 22 . . . June . . .* (State Papers. Session 31 May–13 August 1859. Vol. xxxii. Return to an address (22 July), No. 117). *Further Despatch . . .* (*ibid.* Command Paper No. 2550). The quotation is on p. 567 of the volume.
[2] 13 July (Fitzmaurice, *Granville*, vol. i, pp. 350–1)

the Queen pointing out that this was a device of Napoleon's to enlist England positively against Austria, in order that he himself could appear less antagonistic to her in actual negotiation.[1] When events proved the Queen right—the Emperor's terms at Villafranca were more favourable to Austria than the terms which the two statesmen had been willing to endorse— Palmerston was 'deeply mortified and annoyed'.[2]

For the peace brought an entirely new situation. Whereas at the end of June the Cabinet had based its speculations on the assumption that the whole of North Italy would be liberated, and that the provisional Governments in Central Italy would survive, the agreement of Villafranca left Venetia in Austrian hands and provided for the return of the Grand Duke of Tuscany and the Duke of Modena. Moreover, there was to be an Italian Confederation under the presidency of the Pope, of which Austria, by virtue of her possession of Venetia, would be a member. Palmerston said it was not, as had been promised, ' l'Italie rendue à elle-même ', but ' l'Italie vendue à l'Autriche '. The Queen, however, was delighted at the restorations, and only regretted that the fate of the Duchess of Parma was uncertain.[3]

At first the details of the settlement were unknown. It was, in particular, doubtful whether the use of force was contemplated to bring back the Dukes. In any case the final conditions had been left to a Conference—a meeting of representatives of the Powers immediately concerned—to be held later at Zürich. After that, it was planned to convene a full European Congress to ratify the work of the peace conference. It was by no means obvious how best England

---

[1] A. J. P. Taylor, 'European Mediation and the Agreement of Villafranca', *E.H.R.*, vol. li (1936), pp. 52–78
[2] Fitzmaurice, *Granville*, vol. i, p. 351
[3] Hon. E. Ashley, *The Life of Viscount Palmerston* (London, 1876), vol. ii, p. 166. *QVL*, vol. iii, p. 355

could approach the question of the peace and the Congress : whether she should leave the matter entirely to the former belligerents, or try to modify their decisions ; and, if the latter, whether now, or nearer the time of the Congress. The Queen contended that England must make no attempt to cause the Emperor to break his word. But Palmerston and Russell wished to obtain from him the assurance that he would not permit the use of force to effect the restoration of the Dukes ; they hoped to defeat the project of an Italian confederation, which, said Palmerston, would be ' worse than a suit in Chancery ' ; and they desired to establish for the future the principle of non-intervention in Italian affairs.[1]

Battle was joined over a draft dispatch to Cowley requesting information about the peace, embodying these views, and making England's attendance at a Congress dependent on France's agreeing with them. It also recommended a lay vicariate for the Legations, and a stronger frontier for Piedmont in Lombardy. After much discussion the Cabinet on 23 July, apparently at Grey's suggestion, added a passage which, though it seems to have been understood by Palmerston and Russell to withhold only the remarks about the Congress, could more naturally be construed to mean that the whole dispatch was to be kept back until after the peace had been signed. Cowley therefore communicated none of it officially to the French Government.[2]

The next disputes arose over a draft protesting to France and Austria against the use of force in Italy, and over another

---

[1] See, for example, 24 August, the Queen to Russell (*QVL*, vol. iii, p. 363) ; 18 July, Palmerston to Russell (RP PRO 30/22/20) ; 25 August, Russell to the Dean of Bristol (RP PRO 30/22/13)

[2] *Correspondence relating to the Affairs of Italy, from . . . Villafranca to the Postponement of the Congress* (State Papers. Session 24 January–28 August 1860. Vol. lxviii. Command Paper No. 2609) [from this point referred to as *Correspondence*], pp. 20–2. Fitzmaurice, *Granville*, vol. i, pp. 352–7. *QVL*, ʌol. iii, pp. 364–5

outlining a programme for the pacification of the peninsula. A weakened version of the protest—against ' a return to that system of foreign interference which for upwards of forty years has been the misfortune of Italy and the danger of Europe'—was finally authorised, after at least two revisions by the full Cabinet, at an irregularly summoned meeting on 15 August ; while what Granville called the ' most objectionable' draft redistributing North and Central Italy was stopped by a Cabinet on 29 August. The only concession won by Russell on this last occasion was that the dispatch of 25 July might at length be communicated.[1]

The detailed story of this squabble gives an idea of the various positions. Russell was in fact already considering active intervention on behalf of the Italians. He asked the Prime Minister on 5 August : ' If Austria attempts to carry Florence & Parma by force, are we ready to put our veto on her proceeding ? I think we ought to be. But I don't know what the thirteen would say.'[2] He might well feel doubtful on that point, and for the moment he confined himself to advice. He agreed at this time with his friend and copious correspondent, Hudson, that the most desirable of the feasible solutions of the Italian problem would be to put the son of the Duchess of Parma on the throne of Tuscany. On 9 August Russell passed on this recommendation privately to Cowley.[3] On the same day Palmerston wrote to his Foreign Secretary :

As to Italy, I no Doubt said to the Italians I saw that the Stronger and larger the Kingdom of Piemont could be, the better ; and that what would be the best, if only it were possible which it is

---

[1] *Correspondence*, pp. 51–2. RA J. 22/24, 40, 43 (letters from Granville of 10 and 15 August to the Prince, and from Palmerston of 13 August to the Queen) and 85 (Granville to the Prince, 29 August) [2] BMS
[3] 4 and 5 August, Hudson to Russell (RP PRO 30/22/66). CP F.O. 519/197

not, would be that it should include the Duchies Tuscany & the Legations.

But as we have to deal with Possibilities, the Plan of Tuscany to the Parma Family, & Parma to Piemont would be a very good arrangement Modena going either to the one or to the other.[1]

But, after the Tuscans' vote to dethrone the Grand Duke on 16 August, and after the protest had at last been sent, this proposal was jettisoned. The Prime Minister and Foreign Secretary felt that the time had come for England to make an official stand for annexation, in order to combat Walewski's pronouncement that it was an impossibility. At Palmerston's instance, Russell wrote the ' most objectionable ' draft advocating the cession to Piedmont of all the disputed territories except the Legations, where the Parma family were to be Hereditary Papal Viceroys ![2] The Queen sent back the draft, as :

> There are many points in it to which she cannot but feel the greatest objections. It is unnecessary, however, for her to go into these details, as it is against the principle of England volunteering at this moment the intrusion of a scheme of her own for the redistribution of the territories and Governments of Northern Italy, that she must above all protest.

She insisted that a Cabinet be summoned to see the draft.[3] Russell defended himself, saying that he was merely trying to prevent a future war to impose the restorations. The Queen said that the last war was not finished until the peace had been signed, and that there should be no interference with that process.[4] Palmerston was called in, and concluded that the attitude of the Queen and Prince was ' a Cloak for their real objection to anything that tends to impede the

[1] RP PRO 30/22/20
[2] 19 August, Palmerston to Russell (RP PRO 30/22/20). *Correspondence*, p. 57 (Cowley, 18 August, on Walewski on annexation)
[3] 21 August, to Russell (*QVL*, vol. iii, p. 361)
[4] *ibid.* vol. iii, pp. 361–2

Restoration of the Austrian Archdukes'. 'It is a Quibble to say that Diplomatic suggestions or Representations are Intervention in the sense in which Intervention has been repudiated.' But the Queen had been careful not to stop the dispatch on her responsibility alone ; she had merely questioned whether the Cabinet would approve it, in view of the condition made about the dispatch of 25 July.[1] Palmerston and Russell were compelled to consult their colleagues.

Before composing the offending draft, Russell had asked for Gladstone's opinion, which was that the aggrandisement of Piedmont though not 'an object in itself desirable', 'as matters now stand . . . seems to be the most likely course for averting far worse & more pressing evils ; & I certainly agree in your acceptance of Lord Palmerston's suggestions both as to the Duchies & as to the Legations.' Some other Ministers had been disposed to give Russell the benefit of the doubt ; there was some fear that he might otherwise resign. Argyll wrote from Scotland that ' we should adopt whatever course may be considered the most effective in support of Italian freedom ' ; he favoured an enlarged Piedmont, and was not irrevocably opposed to England's sending a representative to the Congress. Herbert had been alarmed by the stories of royal obstruction which he had heard.[2] But, when it was all over, and the misunderstanding about the dispatch of 25 July had been explained away, and the new draft buried, Gladstone recognised that the Queen had been unnecessarily annoyed, and Herbert admitted that she had been acting on behalf of the Cabinet. Argyll was amazed by the reports he received and feared ' some unheal-able breach ' with Russell. He wrote to Gladstone :

[1] 23 August, Palmerston to Russell (RP PRO 30/22/20)
[2] 19 August, Russell to Gladstone ; 22 August, Gladstone to Russell (GP BM Add MS 44291, ff. 245-8). 27 August, Argyll to Gladstone (GP BM Add MS 44098, f. 198). Fitzmaurice, *Granville*, vol. i, p. 354

As far as I can make out from the newspapers, all goes well in Italy, better probably than it would do, if we interfere too actively. . . .

I look much to you—to keep the peace : because your position in reference to Italy will make it very difficult for Lord John to *persist* in any line you may disapprove.[1]

Granville expounded to the Prince the foreign policy of the majority of the Cabinet, to wit, that :

Our language to Italian Governments ought to show sympathy with Italy, and let them know that we were anxious that they should be left free to act and decide for themselves ; that it should inform them in the clearest manner that in no case were they to obtain active assistance from us, and it ought to avoid giving any advice as to their conduct, which might make us responsible for the evil or danger which might accrue from following such advice. That our language to France and Austria ought to press upon them in every *judicious* manner the expediency of doing that which was likely to secure the permanent happiness of Italy, and to persuade them to abstain from forcing upon the Italians, persons and forms of Government to which they objected ; nothing like a menace or a promise to be used.

At the actual meeting Russell was ' evidently ashamed of much of his own case ', and Palmerston's request ' for fuller powers to act during the recess . . . was met by a general assurance of readiness to come up by night trains.'[2] A few days later Russell wrote to Palmerston :

The Prince says the Queen wishes after we have made our protest & communicated my despatch of the 25 of July, that we should remain quiet, till a decision shall become necessary. I shall be glad to acquiesce in this, as I see that every draft of mine will require a cabinet & that is unpracticable.[3]

[1] *ibid.* vol. i, pp. 356–8. 8th Duke of Argyll, *Autobiography and Memoirs* (London, 1906), vol. ii, pp. 144–55. 3 September, Argyll to Gladstone (GP BM Add MS 44098, ff. 205–07)

[2] 29 August (*QVL*, vol. iii, p. 366). 31 August, Granville to Argyll (Fitzmaurice, *Granville*, vol. i, p. 358)

[3] 5 September (RP PRO 30/22/30)

The Court's and the Cabinet's policy of genuine non-interference had won a notable victory.

Muzzled as regards official dispatches, Palmerston and Russell still found means to make known their views to other Governments. The Prime Minister had several times in private conversations with foreign representatives flouted the wishes of the majority of his Cabinet. Russell was similarly indiscreet. No sooner had the Court and the Cabinet won their struggle for control of official communications than a further quarrel broke out over attempts to circumvent it. As Granville said, 'It is the most dangerous time of year. Palm. will see nobody but Toadies. He has no colleagues & no Commons to show him how the wind blows.'[1] On 3 September Palmerston had a long talk with Persigny, the French Ambassador, during the course of which he gave his personal approval to a project, suggested by Persigny on his own initiative, for an alliance between England and France to secure the annexation of the Duchies to Piedmont and the partition of the Pope's dominions between Naples and Piedmont. Palmerston said that he hoped that France would make some such proposition officially ! When the Queen heard of this and other recent private communications— Cowley had referred to one of them in a despatch, and Walewski had complained about them—she embarked on a long constitutional argument with her Prime Minister. She pointed out that he was not merely advocating policies which the Cabinet had not approved ; he was actually suggesting to France that she should make proposals which would, if made, be most embarrassing to England. Palmerston threatened to resign if he was not allowed to discuss all questions fully with diplomats ; and he forced Cowley to

[1] 9 September, to Sir G. Grey (Minister in attendance at Balmoral) (RA J. 23/36)

withdraw the tell-tale dispatch. But the Queen's protest was not ineffectual : Russell comforted her with the information that he thought ' there never was a time when it was less expedient to fetter this country by prospective engagements ; ' and a caution was included in a dispatch of 17 September to Walewski ' against treating as official any proceeding which does not assume the official form, and is not the deliberate expression of the views of Her Majesty's Government '.[1] On this point, too, the Queen had gained a partial victory. For the next six weeks her relations with her Ministers were relatively peaceable.

Palmerston and Russell were in fact now feeling less certain how they should act. They had expressed their wish that the Italians should be left free to settle their own affairs, and they were quite satisfied with the votes of the Central Italian populations in August and September for annexation to Piedmont. But it seemed increasingly unlikely that this solution would prevail : the real intentions of France and Austria were inscrutable ; and the Piedmontese Government, now that Cavour was out of office, was excessively timid. Hudson was always producing some new compromise programme alleged to be the best possible in the circumstances. On 20 August, in the expectation that the Emperor's cousin would be elected ruler of Tuscany, he suggested a bargain with Napoleon to secure the rest of the disputed territory to Piedmont. Palmerston merely pressed the annexation draft all the harder. But when Hudson came to England at the end of September with a plan sponsored by Victor Emanuel, in which the chief emphasis was on the purchase of Venice as a ' compensation ' for the restoration of the Grand Duke of Tuscany, the two Ministers agreed

---

[1] QVL, vol. iii, pp. 367–73. 4 September, Palmerston to Russell (RP PRO 30/22/20). 4 September, Cowley to Palmerston (RA J. 23/24) (also BMS). Fitzmaurice, *Granville*, vol. i, p. 361 (this letter, of 6 September, should be attributed to Sir G. Grey and not General Grey). *Correspondence*, p. 115.

that 'if it could be adopted it would settle Italy for a long time to come.' Even Palmerston's loyalty to the principle of annexation seemed to be wilting.[1]

There were during these months always at least two English policies, one official, one unofficial. Sometimes, owing to the propensity of both Palmerston and Russell for private policy-making, there appeared to be three. About the various proposals for amalgamating the Duchies with Piedmont the two statesmen seemed unable to co-ordinate their views. Palmerston told Azeglio privately on 23 August that a vote for outright annexation would be the best course, and said that he thought Victor Emanuel might well take the risk of accepting the Tuscan offer, even though it would be a great risk. Russell on this occasion was less daring : he advised the King to 'keep order' in Central Italy but to temporise on the actual annexation.[2] When a Regency by the Prince of Carignano on behalf of his brother, Victor Emanuel, was mooted in mid-October, Russell let it be known through Hudson and Panizzi that he favoured the idea. Palmerston, consulted in the last days of the month by Azeglio, declined to give an opinion.[3] Later, when Napoleon had informed the Piedmontese of his disapproval of the Prince's nomination as Regent, Palmerston helped to tone down a dispatch so that England should not promise aid if Carignano agreed to go. Finally, the appointment of Boncompagni, as the deputy for a deputy, welcomed by Palmerston, was criticised by Russell.[4]

[1] 20 August, Hudson to Russell, and Memorandum of 11 September (RP PRO 30/22/66). 29 August and 3 October, Palmerston to Russell (RP PRO 30/22/20)

[2] ed. Colombo, *Carteggi inediti di E. d'Azeglio*, vol. ii, p. 213. 27 August, Russell to Cowley (CP F.O. 519/197)

[3] ed. Colombo, *Carteggi inediti di E. d'Azeglio*, vol. ii, pp. 233-7. Brooks, *Panizzi*, pp. 213-15

[4] 11 November, Palmerston to Russell (RP PRO 30/22/20). 15 October, Azeglio to Dabormida (ed. Colombo, *Carteggi inediti di E. d'Azeglio*, vol. ii, pp. 241-2)

III

At the party meeting in June Palmerston had committed himself and his Government very explicitly to neutrality; and for some time there was no talk of departing from this pledge. But, as has already been stated, Russell was thinking of intervening actively on behalf of the Italians as early as 5 August; and on 3 September Palmerston was agreeing with Persigny that France and England should ally over Italy. It is true that Palmerston had also committed the Government, at the party meeting, to the French alliance. But clearly there had not then been any expectation that England might agree to join France in giving material support to the Italians. This possibility, however, was being seriously discussed in Cabinet from November 1859 to January 1860.

During the Crimean War England and France had been allies in the ordinary sense, united against Russia. Subsequently they had drifted apart. But it was still felt that some sort of alliance existed between them, and that it ought to be strengthened. The relationship was certain to be ambivalent. Although Napoleon had assured the world time and time again that he was determined to stand well with England, it could not be overlooked that he was ruler of the strongest state on the Continent of Europe and that he had an obvious interest in upsetting the Treaties of 1815, perhaps to the point when England would feel bound to fight against him. The basic purpose of Palmerston and other advocates of the French alliance—among whom were Disraeli, Gladstone, Cowley, and even Malmesbury and Clarendon—was to take advantage of the Emperor's sentimental attachment to the English connexion in order to moderate his policy as much as possible to suit English views. There was no confidence that Napoleon would always stay at peace with a Power whose interests were so likely to clash with his and the French nation's ambitions. But it was believed that, the closer the alliance, the less probable the quarrel. There was a further argument: it would be very convenient to England, pledged to neutrality and poorly armed on land, to be able to exercise a degree of control over the actions of a country with an army as powerful as the French.[1]

At first sight it may not be easy to see how the French alliance, desirable though it might be on general grounds, came to be the hope of Italophiles. Historians have emphasised that England promoted the liberation of Italy partly in order to create a counterpoise to France; and there is no doubt that Villafranca made some Englishmen more willing to assist the Italians, simply because it made that course seem no longer identical with furthering French aggrandisement. But this is not the whole story. It was a paradoxical situation. The English Government was committed to neutrality, and in any event had not the means at its disposal to intervene on its own account against Austria in Italy. If, as seemed to be the case, Austria was ready to fight to restore the Central Italian Dukes, it was plainly not going to be sufficient for England to express in a dispatch, still less for Palmerston or Russell to state in a private communication, an opinion in favour of the emancipation of Italy. The only Power which might be prepared to adopt England's Italian policy, and supply the force to carry it into effect, with or without an actual alliance, was France. So, while one of England's motives for supporting the Italians was the wish to reduce French influence in the peninsula, the fact had to be faced that this end could be

[1] I have read M. A. Anderson, 'The Character of British Relations with France, 1859–1865' (unpublished M.A. dissertation, London University, 1949). It deals with the French alliance in general, but not in detail with its relation to Italian policy.

achieved only with French help. In trying to strengthen the French alliance, therefore, Palmerston and Russell had the delicate task of persuading Napoleon to act against what they conceived to be his interests in Italy. Their principal assets were Napoleon's personal sympathy with Italian nationalism and his desire for friendship with England. Their liabilities included the rooted opposition of the Court and the Cabinet, and probably the country too.

During the summer and autumn both English and French statesmen put forward tentative suggestions for closer association. Palmerston and Russell tried to commit France to annexation as a basis of agreement. The Emperor hinted that he welcomed English advocacy of such a policy because he wished to find a way of releasing himself from his engagements at Villafranca. Persigny, as has been seen, made a proposal to Palmerston on 3 September. The result of that particular overture was not encouraging : Walewski disowned it, and the Emperor endorsed Walewski by refusing to accept his resignation ; while Russell said ' that no such proposition ought to be made to our government at this moment '.[1] But the completion of the work of the Zürich conference on 17 October was soon followed by the first official feelers from Napoleon.

After much discussion in mid-October, the English Government was slowly coming to the conclusion that it could not be represented at the coming Congress : the Zürich terms—a mere rehash of Villafranca—were too unsatisfactory. But on 28 October Russell, fortified by a new pronouncement from Walewski that France, although she still desired the restorations, would not countenance the use of force to procure them, provisionally recommended to the Cabinet acceptance of the invitation. It was finally agreed to promise ' fair con-

[1] 7 September, to Palmerston (RP PRO 30/22/30)

sideration' for it, and England proposed that the thrones of the Dukes should be acknowledged vacant, in order to make the votes for annexation valid. This Walewski rejected.[1] But the rapprochement continued. Cavour, whose opinion Russell had sought, begged England to accede to the Congress, for the sake of the Italian cause.[2] France would need some supporter there unless she was to bow irrevocably to Austria's wishes. It was arguable that England, as a Great Power, ought in any case to be present at such a meeting. Moreover, Austria now declared that she would regard the appearance of Piedmontese soldiers in Central Italy as a *casus belli*.[3] Something like the situation of a year earlier seemed to be developing. To Palmerston and Russell the remedy was clear : England and France must this time show their solidarity. If Russell did now what Malmesbury should have done, according to the Liberals, in the spring, war might be averted.[4] Part of the reason for English willingness to join more closely with France at this stage was the necessity of winning her co-operation in disputes in China and Morocco.[5] But the chief incentive was the critical state of the Italian Question.

Cowley transmitted a specific suggestion from Napoleon on 17 November. The Emperor said he was encountering great difficulties in carrying out the programme he had always had at heart, the emancipation of Italy ; and he would like to concert with England a settlement which could be reasonably offered to Austria. He did not regard annexation as practicable, but thought a separate Central Italian Kingdom

[1] ed. Gooch, *Later Correspondence of Russell*, vol. ii, pp. 244–8. *Correspondence*, pp. 149–51, and 164–5. RA J. 23/85–91

[2] 24 October, Cavour to Panizzi (ed. Fagan, *Lettere ad A. Panizzi*, pp. 379–82). 2 November, Russell to Palmerston (BMS)

[3] e.g. 29 November, Cowley to Russell (*Correspondence*, p. 222)

[4] See 7 September, Russell to the Queen (*QVL*, vol. iii, p. 370)

[5] See Palmerston-Russell correspondence (RP PRO 30/22/20)

might be formed, under a new dynasty.[1] Palmerston welcomed the scheme as a possible compromise which England might support if annexation could not be carried out. Russell saw in it a great opportunity. 'I am very anxious,' he told Cowley, 'if possible, to come to an understanding with the Emperor before the Congress meets.' To Palmerston he wrote : 'If we can save Italy from dependence & Europe from war I shall not break my heart if we do a favour to Napoleon at the same time.'[2] The Queen, though she at first described the scheme as ' the often attempted one, that England should take the chestnuts out of the fire, and assume the responsibility of drawing the Emperor Napoleon from his engagements', and though she emphatically did not wish for a secret understanding with France, admitted on 22 November that she thought 'the plan Ld Cowley sketches out for the settlt. of the Italian question, much the most feasible one'.[3]

Cabinet opposition proved too strong for the proposal of an understanding with France. 'Not one sentence of his draft was left unaltered', so Lewis and Newcastle told the Prince. But Russell was permitted to say to Napoleon, in a dispatch of 26 November, that, as a second-best solution, England would not oppose the establishment of an independent Central Italian Kingdom, preferably under a prince of the House of Savoy. There was to be no mention of the possibility of English armed intervention.[4] The Foreign Secretary, however, grew more and more enthusiastic for the alliance. After a probing letter from the Queen, he announced on 1 December

[1] RA J. 23/124. See Martin, *Life of the Prince Consort*, vol. iv, pp. 506–07
[2] 18 November, Palmerston to Russell (RP PRO 30/22/20). 19 November (CP F.O. 519/197) to Cowley and (BMS) to Palmerston
[3] 18 November, to Russell (Martin, *Life of the Prince Consort*, vol. iv, p. 507). To Russell (RP PRO 30/22/13)
[4] Memorandum by Albert, 24 November (RA J. 23/135). *Correspondence*, pp. 212–13. This seems to be the occasion of which Wood speaks later, when ' we struck out " material support " ' (Wood to General Grey, (?)8 December, J. 24/38).

that he was ' certainly not prepared to say that a case might not arise when the interests of Great Britain might require that she should give material support to the Emperor of the French ', though he considered ' the fear of such an alliance will prevent Austria from disturbing the peace of Europe '.[1] Three days later, Palmerston and Persigny had another private conversation, the substance of which Palmerston put into writing : he had again urged the French to give their assent to annexation. Persigny replied sympathetically, but suggesting that England, to demonstrate her friendship, should propose that France, as her compensation for the aggrandisement of Piedmont, might take Savoy ! Even Palmerston regarded that idea as ' dashing '. Russell rejected it, but continued with his plans for the alliance.[2] He informed Cowley that ' I agree with the Emperor & with you, but there is no getting an English cabinet to exercise foresight. I doubt however even if I had my own way whether I would commit the country to annexation. If a mezzo-Termine, not *so* disagreeable to Austria can be found, I am disposed to accept it.' [3] With Palmerston he was not so forthright :

One difficulty only on the subject of annexation, but that a great one, strikes me. It is *the* plan which Austria is pledged by declarations and hatred to oppose. If we urge it upon the French Emperor, as you do, in your letter to Persigny, are we not bound, if he accepts and supports it . . . to stand by him ? I am ready to accept this responsibility, and I suppose you are. It would be Belgium and Spain over again. But the Cabinet is not at present prepared to go to that length. Therefore I should say

1. Propose annexation as the clear decision of Central Italy.
2. Profess ourselves (that rejected), to be ready to lend our aid in recommending a compromise in Central Italy.

[1] *QVL*, vol. iii, p. 374
[2] 6 December, Palmerston to Russell (RP PRO 30/22/20). 7 December, Russell to Palmerston (BMS) [3] 6 December (CP F.O. 519/197)

3. Compromise rejected, let us be ready to join France and Sardinia in supporting annexation. Compromise accepted, Austria must take it.[1]

But royal and Cabinet opposition deferred the matter for the moment. Wood said the Cabinet only awaited the opportunity to enter in a dispatch a clear opinion against any use of force by England.[2]

In the first days of January the project of an alliance was thoroughly debated, and defeated. It was not again put to the Cabinet. The discussion was as revealing as its result was decisive. On 20 December Russell composed and sent to Palmerston the 'Draft of a secret dispatch to Cowley which I think is necessary, but it may meet obstructions of which you are aware. We are coming to the final decision between light and darkness. Happily Austria who holds the brief of Darkness is very weak just now.'[3] Over the next fortnight Palmerston and Russell discussed the exact form which their proposal should take. At first it was a promise of a triple alliance between England, France and Piedmont if Austria attacked in Italy; then it became a triple alliance to forestall an Austrian attack. A Cabinet was fixed for 3 January, to consider some such proposition. Cowley came to London to support the alliance. The Queen and Prince of course objected violently, and warned their sympathisers in the Cabinet.[4]

Meanwhile, developments in France favoured the alliance. On 22 December appeared another of Napoleon's 'inspired' pamphlets, called *Le Pape et le Congrès*, which was the culmination of a series of hints that he was nerving himself to break

[1] 7 December (BMS)
[2] Wood to General Grey already quoted, RA J. 24/38, (?)8 December
[3] BMS
[4] See RP PRO 30/22/20, and 21 at the turn of the year, Granville refers to the 'Prince's note' when reporting the Cabinet of 3 January (RA J. 24/86). 5 January, Memorandum by Cowley (F.O. 27/1331).

with Rome.[1] The tract denied that the Pope needed a temporal dominion extending beyond the boundaries of the Eternal City, and argued that France should no longer be responsible for perpetuating this monstrosity. On 21 December Napoleon had assured Cobden, who had been for some time negotiating privately for a commercial treaty with France, that ' he had quite made up his mind to enter into the Treaty, and that the only question was as to the details '.[2] Hitherto only Gladstone of the English Ministers had seriously entertained the idea, and some knew nothing of it. Now the Cabinet could, and must, be informed. On 4 January Walewski was at last to be replaced by Thouvenel, formerly Ambassador at Constantinople. The Emperor had in fact decided on a complete change of policy, the results of which were to include the postponement and eventual abandonment of the Congress (because Austria demanded a disavowal of the pamphlet as a condition of her attendance), and the return to power of Cavour. Though the full extent of the change was not appreciated by the time the Cabinet met, it was already plain that the Emperor was willing to make considerable concessions in the hope of capturing the English alliance.

At the Cabinet :

Johnny, backed by Pam, by Gladstone, and partially by Milner Gibson, Somerset and Argyll, proposed to pledge ourselves to France that we would give material assistance to France if Austria used force in Italy. Cardwell and Elgin, as usual, gave no opinion. The rest of us objected strongly. The Cabinet adjourned for a week.[3]

Apparently the firm opposition surprised Palmerston and

[1] The most notable of these hints was a speech on 11 October in reply to remarks of the Cardinal-Archbishop of Bordeaux. See L. M. Case, *French Opinion on War and Diplomacy during the Second Empire* (Philadelphia, 1954), p. 105.   [2] Morley, *Cobden*, p. 721
[3] 17 January, Granville to Canning (Fitzmaurice, *Granville*, vol. i, p. 369)

Russell. The Prime Minister had said that ' What you intend to propose . . . seems to be quite safe, and as much probably as our Colleagues would be willing to agree to.' He suggested the adjournment ' because the Dissenting Members were not likely to be convinced on the Sudden, and a weeks delay will give time for better Consideration, but the Case is so clear that I cannot doubt their coming round to our opinions.'[1] He immediately embarked on a campaign to persuade the doubters, circulating a long memorandum and writing ' to several of us, telling us that Johnny would resign, and that he entirely agreed with Johnny. We, without concert, wrote the same sort of firm answers.'[2]

From Windsor on the night of 3 January, however, Gladstone sent an enormous letter to Russell supporting the proposal. He argued particularly that, for the Central Italian populations, further delay of a settlement would be intolerable. He thought therefore that the question must be decided quickly. Moreover, the sooner England committed herself, the safer and more successful her action was likely to be, since she might thereby prevent the combination of the Powers opposed to her views, whether in the Congress or in resort to force. He did not regard the suggested move as a threat of war ; he considered that it would not bring war nearer, but could only tend to reduce its probability ; and he believed that the Emperor could in this matter be relied upon. The situation had altered since the Cabinet had last rejected a similar proposal. France had become more amenable, and :

Austria has shown what indeed could hardly be doubted, that she meant to feel her way, and to proceed as far as she could in this direction [i.e. towards the use of force]. Russia and Prussia have

[1] 2 and 4 January, to Russell (RP PRO 30/22/21)
[2] Fitzmaurice, *Granville*, vol. i, p. 369—the letter already quoted

shown by their answers to our overtures that they will give us no right to count on their co-operation. . . . Above all the Pope has been brought into the field. . . .

Gladstone took it for granted, however, that Piedmont, as well as France and Austria, must be forbidden to intervene in Central Italy. In general, he favoured the French alliance ' as the true basis of peace in Europe (for England and France never will unite in any European purpose which is radically unjust) ', and thought this proposal ' prudent as well as bold ' :

leaving open the question what the precise form should be, but hoping that it will be one that may involve closer union with France for what now clearly appears to be a common object, and a more distinct and developed affirmation of the principle we have adopted from the first that foreign force ought no longer to be used as the instrument of government in Central Italy.[1]

Palmerston's arguments in his great memorandum of 5 January were somewhat similar. He emphasised that it was desirable to come to an arrangement with France before the sympathisers with Austria could co-ordinate their action. He repudiated isolationism : ' Austria does not trust thus to the chapter of accidents.' The projected alliance ' would better deserve the title of holy alliance than the league which bore that name.'

But such an engagement might lead us into war. War with whom ? War with Austria. Well, suppose it did, would that war be one of great effort and expense ? Clearly not. France, Sardinia, and Central Italy would furnish troops more than enough to repel any attempt which Austria could make to coerce Sardinia or Central Italy. Our share in such a war would be chiefly, if not wholly, naval ; and our squadron in the Adriatic

---

[1] GP BM Add MS 44291, ff. 286–95. (Also in RP PRO 30/22/19) This letter has been published, from the British Museum version, in D. Beales, ' Gladstone on the Italian Question ', *Rass. stor. del Ris.*, vol. xli (1954), pp. 99–104.

would probably be the utmost of our contribution. . . . But is such a war likely ? On the contrary, it is in the highest degree probable that such an engagement between England, France, and Sardinia would be the most effectual means of preventing a renewal of war in Italy.

Palmerston was thinking specifically in terms of a triple alliance; Gladstone seems to have considered only an agreement with France. But they both expressed great fervour in support of the principle. Gladstone said ' we ought cheerfully to stake in so noble and great a cause the existence of an Administration ; ' and Palmerston ' would far rather give up office for maintaining the principle on which the course which I recommend would be founded, than retain office by giving that principle up.' [1]

It should be observed that the whole of Palmerston's case for a French alliance was not set out in this memorandum. There is no reference to the need to restrain France. Yet at no time had Palmerston forgotten the possibility of French aggression against England. On 7 August 1859 he had written to Russell :

One thing Experience has shewn us, & that is that Napoleon broods for years over an Idea, and sooner or later tries to carry it out ; and we all know that some years ago and before he became Emperor one of his fixed Ideas was to wipe out Waterloo by the Humiliation of England. . . . He hardly knows himself how he may feel Six or Twelve Months Hence. [2]

On 11 October he thought : ' It is plain that France aims, through Spain, at getting fortified points on each side of the Gut of Gibraltar . . . and thus virtually to shut us out of the Mediterranean.' [3] And on 4 November :

[1] Ashley, *Palmerston*, vol. ii, pp. 174–80   [2] RP PRO 30/22/20
[3] Ashley, *Palmerston*, vol. ii, p. 166

Till lately I had strong confidence in the fair intentions of Napoleon towards England, but of late I have begun to feel great distrust. . . .

He has been assiduously labouring to increase his naval means, evidently for offensive as well as defensive purposes ; and latterly great pains have been taken to raise throughout France . . . hatred of England. . . . All this may be explained away . . . ; but it would be unwise in any English Government to shut its eyes to all these symptoms. . . . Of course we should take as ' argent comptant ' all their professions of ' alliance intime et durable ' . . .; and the only expression we ought to give of anything like suspicion should be in the activity and scale of our defensive arrangements.[1]

When he wrote to Clarendon in defence of Russell's proposal on 4 January 1860, he pointed out that, if England chose allies by the mischief they might do her, ' Austria could do us no possible harm as an enemy : France could injure us seriously.' [2] And he had told Russell on 26 December :

I should be quite ready for your triple alliance ; it would effectually accomplish its Purpose, and without the slightest chance of bringing on a war it would moreover remove to a greater Distance that Rupture with France which sooner or later must be looked to as a possible if not probable Event.[3]

Russell had replied that he did ' not see why, if we act with France in the Italian Question, we may not put off *sine die* the French war '.[4] These considerations, however, Palmerston and Russell kept to themselves for the moment.

The ' firm answers ' to Palmerston's memorandum employed a wide range of arguments. Argyll had not felt ' quite sure of the immediate *necessity* of the step you proposed ', though he said he would have voted for it. He continued to emphasise this point :

[1] *ibid.* vol. ii, pp. 187–9   [2] Maxwell, *Clarendon*, vol. ii, p. 199
[3] RP PRO 30/22/20   [4] 27 December (BMS)

So far as I know, there never has been any question as to the expediency of coming to an understanding with France as to the line we shd take in Congress.

Neither has there been any doubt as to what that line should be . . . Non-Intervention. . . .

The only question has been Shall we engage, *beforehand*, to support this Policy by force of arms ?

This Engagement cannot be opposed on the ground that we may leave France to get out of the scrape as best she can. We are bound to support the Independence of Italy : and if it were seriously threatened, we *could not* now remain passive spectators of the contest. . . .

The proposed Engagement is in the interests of Peace. I believe it to be safe in itself—so safe, that the only doubt I have is, whether it is *necessary* ?

If it is understood that ' Foreign ' intervention is to exclude equally *all* Foreign intervention—Sardinian as well as Austrian,— it will be still more clearly an Engagement to preserve the Peace of Europe.[1]

What he feared emerges from a letter to Gladstone :

One thing I am sure of—that nothing but absolute necessity will justify our taking any step which will involve serious danger to Palmerston's Govt. The influence of His name, combined with Ld. John's and your own, is of itself a tower of strength to the Italian cause. . . .

Seeing the strong reluctance of the Cabinet, and knowing the feeling elsewhere in favour of non-entanglement in formal engagements, I think the proposal should not be pressed, *unless*, and *until* we are sure that the success of the Italian cause is in more serious danger than it is just now.[2]

Somerset also favoured the general idea. ' It seems improbable that the Emperor of the French will much longer be content to

---

[1] The long quotation is from BMS, not dated, (?) 5 or 6 January. The short one from a letter to Russell of 3 January (RP PRO 30/22/25).
[2] 5 January (GP BM Add MS 44098, ff.250–1)

remain in his present isolated position. If he cannot form a closer alliance with England, he will unite in some way or other with Russia or with Austria.'[1] Gladstone naturally agreed with Palmerston's memorandum, though he expressed 'especial concurrence' in remarks made by others on the need for the continuance of the existing Cabinet.[2] But Lewis thought that, 'without some overt act on the part of Austria, we cannot properly [enter] into a written engagement with France to guarantee the provinces of Central Italy against foreign intervention.'[3] Wood saw no English interest involved.[4] Grey and Campbell were opposed to the plan.[5] Herbert advised waiting until the Congress was definitely abandoned, and raised one or two difficult questions : would the Pope, for example, if he could do it single-handed, be allowed to reconquer the Romagna ? But he approved the proposal in principle.[6] Granville hoped Russell would accept some modification of the original suggestion :

I believe that while many of the Cabinet entertain insuperable objections to our engaging ourselves to give material assistance, all or nearly all are ready to agree to great moral support to France and to strong moral pressure upon Austria in order to prevent armed interference in Italy ; in short, that independent and unfettered policy by which Lord John has hitherto succeeded in preventing Italy from being bullied either by France or Austria.[7]

Clarendon, consulted by Palmerston, and informed by Lewis and Villiers, said he doubted the benefit to England of annexation, which would merely enlarge the size of an inevitably pro-French state. He knew that on 7 January ' the government is in extreme peril from internal combustion.'

[1] 5 January, BMS   [2] 7 January, BMS
[3] 7 January, BMS   [4] 7 January, BMS
[5] Long memorandum by Grey in RP PRO 30/22/25, dated 9 January. Maxwell, *Clarendon*, vol. ii, p. 202   [6] 10 January, BMS
[7] 7 January, to Palmerston (Fitzmaurice, *Granville*, vol. i, p. 368)

The present intention of Pam., J.R. and Gladstone is to cram this policy down the throats of their twelve colleagues, and, if they won't swallow it, to resign : if they *will* swallow it and the H. of Commons *won't*, then to dissolve parliament. But three dissolutions in three years is what the country won't swallow, so that either way the government will come to an end, unless the three knock under. Until the contrary is a *fait accompli*, I shall continue to expect a patch up, tho' it will be a hollow one, for I imagine Johnny is getting sick of the humiliations he has had to endure, and of others which are in store for his conceit. . . .

[The Queen] in the event of the Cabinet agreeing to Pam.'s policy and requiring that it should be indicated in the speech from the throne . . . would refuse point blank to do so, let the consequences be what they might.

Clarendon's own special objection to the scheme was this : that it was just at the time when Napoleon most needed English assistance to counter-balance his loss of Catholic support that Palmerston was trying to commit England to him, thereby throwing away a commanding advantage.[1] Curiously enough, Cobden, who was also in the secret by virtue of his negotiations for a commercial treaty, made exactly the same point.[2]

Persigny was the author of the suggestion that broke the deadlock. He proposed that for the present, instead of forming an actual alliance with France, England should merely ask both France and Austria to agree that neither should interfere in Italy. Palmerston welcomed the idea : ' The more I think of Persigny's suggestion the more it seems to me calculated as an immediate move to get over Cabinet Difficulties.' [3] Russell soon acquiesced. And almost all the other members of the

[1] To the Duchess of Manchester (Maxwell, *Clarendon*, vol. ii, pp. 206–07). cf. 8 January, Clarendon to Palmerston (*ibid.* vol. ii, pp. 200–01)

[2] Morley, *Cobden*, p. 727

[3] 7 January, Russell to Palmerston (BMS). 9 January, Palmerston to Russell (RP PRO 30/22/20)

Cabinet were obviously hoping for some compromise. So, at the meeting on 10 January :

> Johnny read an irrelevant letter from Augustus Loftus, and said : ' I think, therefore, without departing from anything which I said the other day, that our best course will now be to ask the Emperors of the French and of Austria whether they would not both agree to abstain from armed interference in Italy.' The relief on some of the countenances, particularly that of Jock Campbell, was amusing.[1]

Loftus' letter was not in fact irrelevant, as it contained a statement of his ' impression' that Austria would not risk using force in Italy again. But this hardly mattered. The fear that the Cabinet might break up counted for much more. So the crisis ' vanished into thin air,' the Queen and Prince not daring to oppose the new plan.[2] It was embodied in a dispatch of 15 January, which also recommended French withdrawal from Rome, the abandonment of attempts to impose reforms in Venetia, and a second plebiscite in the Duchies.[3]

Honours were divided. The Court, though still most perturbed, was relieved of its worst anxieties. The Cabinet had again shown its extreme reluctance—despite all Palmerston's wiles and Napoleon's blandishments—to offer material support to France or to the Italians. On the other hand, according to Granville : ' Nearly all admitted, except Mr. Villiers, Sir Charles Wood, & myself, that it might be necessary to join France in war, but said that it was too early to pledge ourselves.'[4] The two ' Italian' statesmen might therefore claim a partial victory.

---

[1] 17 January, Granville to Canning (Fitzmaurice, *Granville*, vol. i, p. 369)
[2] 11 January, Clarendon to Lewis (Maxwell, *Clarendon*, vol. ii, p. 204)
[3] Walpole, *Russell*, vol. ii, pp. 315–16 ; *Further Correspondence . . . Italy. Part II* (State Papers. Session 24 January–28 August 1860. Vol. lxvii. Command Paper No. 2636), p. 4
[4] 3 January, to the Prince Consort (RA J. 24/86)

It must be made clear that neither the original proposal nor the ultimate compromise embodied the principle of self-determination in Italy, at least in the strict sense. During the discussions it was never settled whether the alliance was to be based on acceptance of the votes for annexation or whether the former Duchies were to be united into an independent Central Italian Kingdom. Cowley's messages from Napoleon, and Cowley himself, had not advocated annexation. The Emperor seems to have intended, as Cowley certainly did, to propose the establishment of a separate state. Cowley and Palmerston had a violent correspondence on the subject, the Ambassador saying that he thought annexation impossible and undesirable from the point of view of English interests, the Prime Minister ridiculing the notion that France would control Piedmont if all North and Central Italy were annexed.[1] Russell was toying with a scheme for a confederation, which Palmerston called setting up 'a little nest of Republics in Central Italy'.[2] Gladstone, in a conversation with the Prince Consort, acknowledged—before he saw Palmerston's memorandum—that he understood the proposal on this occasion, unlike that 'put and not pressed about a month ago', to prohibit Piedmont as well as other Powers from intervention in Central Italy :

That what was now proposed was an engagement to resist the use of foreign force in Central Italy—That according to the natural meaning of the proposal, . . . it implied that the Pope might recover the allegiance of his revolted subjects.—That they, and doubtless the people of Tuscany and the Duchies who are in the same boat, might baffle him if they could—but that no one else should interfere—and I admitted that Sardinia could make no title on any ground of European law, or any recognised principle of

[1] BMS, esp. Cowley to Palmerston, 23 January. See 27 January, Clarendon to Cowley (CP F.O. 519/178)
[2] 22 December, to Russell (RP PRO 30/22/20)

policy to interfere in the strife, which would not also entail and justify the interference of Austria.[1]

Herbert and Russell bore Gladstone out on the nature of the proposal, and agreed in preferring it to annexation. Argyll's concurring opinion has already been quoted. What confused the issue was Palmerston's faithfulness to the principle of annexation, which Russell seemed to share at the meetings of the Cabinet.[2] But the point was settled in the compromise dispatch, when the majority of the Ministers had it stipulated, against the wishes of Palmerston and Russell, that a second plebiscite be held in the Duchies.[3]

IV

During their first seven months of office the Liberal Ministers were subjected to no great pressure from Parliament or the public. At the time of year when the Cabinet was appointed, in mid-June, the Parliamentary session would normally have been well advanced ; and, despite the loss of so many days as a result of the Election and the political crisis, neither the Government nor the Opposition wished to bring up further controversial business. So it proved possible to terminate the session formally on 13 August, by which time many Members were already on the moors. There had indeed been some discussion of foreign affairs. A handful of dispatches for which Peers and M.P.s had asked had been published ; and a lively debate had taken place on 8 August in the House of Commons, on a motion which sought to restrain the Government from participating in the

[1] 6 January, Gladstone to Palmerston : ed. P. Guedalla, *Gladstone and Palmerston* (London, 1928), pp. 120-1
[2] 27 January, Clarendon to Cowley (CP F.O. 519/178)
[3] 13 January, Granville to the Prince Consort (RA J. 25/24)

proposed Congress. But the Ministry had refused to give the more important dispatches in the first instance, and only produced them after they had already appeared in the Press ; while the motion of 8 August was not brought to a division, the previous question being successfully moved.[1] Like the Conservatives early in 1859, the Liberals after the peace of Villafranca were confronted with an entirely new international situation in which negotiation was all-important. They had the initiative in policy-making ; and they had good justification for being discreet. Palmerston's Administration was more fortunate than Derby's in that it was free of Parliament for five crucial months. Apart from a few public speeches, in breaks from grouse and deer—such as Russell's at Aberdeen on 28 September, Lewis's at the Guildhall on 9 November, and others by Ministers in their own constituencies—the Government had to make no pronouncements on foreign policy between 8 August and 24 January, when Parliament reassembled.[2] Its worst embarrassment of these months was *The Times'* violent articles against the French alliance early in January, articles which must have been inspired either from within the Cabinet or by someone like Clarendon with inside knowledge.[3]

This was the sole occasion during the recess when Ministers took serious account of the probable reaction of public opinion to their foreign policy. They could, of course, only guess ; and the guesses varied considerably. Palmerston claimed that his proposal ' would be highly approved ', and that, if the Cabinet broke up on the question, he and his supporters ' would stand very well before the country '.[4] Somerset

[1] *Parl. Deb.*, 3rd series, vol. cliv, cols. 873-7, 881-9, 946-7, 1281-92, 1363-70 ; vol. clv, cols. 31, 542, 1120-1243
[2] *The Times*, 1 October, 10 November, etc.
[3] *The Times*, 6 January, etc.
[4] 5 January, Cabinet Memorandum of Palmerston (Ashley, *Palmerston*, vol. ii, p. 180) ; 12 January, Memorandum by the Prince Consort (RA J. 25/17)

thought that 'a good scheme well managed' would be popular.[1] And Gladstone wrote to Russell :

No doubt [public opinion] would be unlikely to follow us were we going to repeat the experiment of the war of last spring which was believed to be a war of aggression on the part of France.

But the public opinion of this country has during the last year moved rapidly and steadily in favour of the Italians. It is now on their side : and when the Englishman has taken his side he loves measures of decision. . . .

The country has emphatically approved the principle announced by you and by Sir G. Lewis at the Guildhall, that we were opposed to forcing a Government upon Central Italy. I believe that if we take the measures most likely to give effect to that principle of action, we shall have its support.[2]

Though Argyll thought that a sudden announcement of an Anglo-French alliance would startle the unsuspecting public, he believed that the situation might alter :

Suspicion and jealousy of France has, till very lately, been the prevalent feeling and has completely overborne the sympathy which, otherwise, would exist for Italy.

Lately—since the peace, this feeling has been subsiding. I am satisfied that if Austria attempted violence again in Italy, the feeling for Italy wd immediately rise in this country, and help the Government in its course.[3]

Herbert, on the other hand, contended that the nation would back only a policy of genuine non-intervention.[4] Outside the Cabinet, Clarendon, Greville and Cobden were convinced

---

[1] 5 January, to Palmerston (BMS)
[2] 3 January (GP BM Add MS 44291, ff.289–90)
[3] 6 January, to Russell (RP PRO 30/22/25)
[4] 10 January, to Palmerston (BMS)

that the alliance would be thoroughly unpopular.[1] The triumvirate was relying on a different trend of opinion from the Cabinet majority. Both trends were clearly strong. It depended on the turn of future events, which would emerge dominant.

[1] 10 January, Clarendon to Greville (*The Greville Memoirs*, vol. viii, p. 282) ; 15 January, Greville to Reeve (ed. A. H. Johnson, *Letters of Charles Greville and Henry Reeve*, 1836–65 (London, 1924), p. 272) ; Morley, *Cobden*, p. 726

Chapter VI

Savoy and Garibaldi

February to December, 1860

RELATIONS with France continued to be the overriding concern of English foreign policy for most of the year 1860. But the prospect of an Anglo-French alliance quickly disappeared. For on 1 March Napoleon III publicly confirmed the persistent rumours that he intended to annex Savoy and Nice. The Italian Question became again for English statesmen, what it had been before July 1859, little more than ' a phrase blazoned on a French banner '.

I

In this phase of the crisis the difficulties of policy-making were enhanced—as are those of the historian—by the fact that the domestic and foreign questions of 1860 were closely inter-related. In Gladstone's words :

Rarely, if ever, in the course of our history has there been such a mixture of high considerations, legislative, military, commercial, foreign, and constitutional, each for the most part traversing the rest, and all capable of exercising a vital influence on public policy, as in the long and complicated session of 1860. The commercial treaty first struck the keynote of the year ; and the most deeply marked and peculiar feature of the year was the silent conflict

131

between the motives and provisions of the treaty on the one hand, and the excitement and exasperation of military sentiment on the other.[1]

Despite the failure of the alliance proposal, the commercial treaty negotiations had continued. Gladstone advocated the treaty vigorously in Cabinet, for reasons which he explained to Graham on 16 January :

We have been employed upon special means of drawing closer our amicable relations with France. To promote this has been for the last few months I may almost say the operation for which I have been living. I have seen in it not merely the increase of influence for a peaceable settlement of the Italian question, not merely the extension—almost the consummation—of the tariff reforms begun in 1842, but also the means of allaying the passions that menace danger, and of shaming the fears which in my opinion have done us much discredit.[2]

By the end of January the main provisions of the treaty had been settled, and it was signed.[3] Gladstone made his great speech in the House of Commons introducing his Budget, which incorporated the tariff changes necessary to implement the treaty, on 10 February ; and on 24 February the Government's majority on the principle of the financial scheme was 116.[4]

Palmerston, however, also had a 'favourite measure' : the strengthening of English military and naval, and particularly coastal, defences. One of the factors contributing to the invasion panic was alarm at France's naval preparations, and especially at her experiments with iron-clad warships. While

[1] W. E. Gladstone, 'The History of 1852–60, and Greville's Latest Journals', *E.H.R.*, vol. ii (1887), p. 296, quoted in Morley, *Gladstone*, vol. ii, p. 1   [2] Parker, *Graham*, vol. ii, p. 392
[3] For details see Morley, *Cobden*, esp. p. 731
[4] See A. L. Dunham, *The Anglo-French Treaty of Commerce of 1860 and the Progress of the Industrial Revolution in France* (Michigan, 1930), esp. pp. 117–21

he was preparing his Budget, Gladstone was faced with demands from his colleagues for fresh expenditure on the Army, on the Navy and on the Navy's bases ; and further demands were made during the spring and summer of 1860. The announcement that the Emperor intended to annex Savoy and Nice helped the alarmists. But the Chancellor resisted vehemently. A bitter conflict in the Cabinet was prolonged throughout most of the session. Not until 23 July could Palmerston introduce his fortifications scheme in the Commons.[1]

With the Budget, the Savoy affair, the defence estimates and the fortifications scheme, Parliament found itself mainly occupied with questions bearing upon foreign policy. The other principal issue of the year, Reform, was overshadowed by these. In fact, from Gladstone's point of view, the Reform Bill served primarily to delay :

the *tail* of the financial measures until a time when the marriage effected by the treaty between England and France had outlived its Parliamentary honeymoon. There had intervened the Savoy and Nice explosion ; . . . French invasion was apprehended by many men usually rational. The Paper Duty bill, which would have passed the Commons by a large majority in the beginning of March, only escaped defeat on May 8 by a majority of nine.[2]

Once Napoleon had broached the annexation question, the Government was faced with a movement of Parliamentary and public opinion against France so strong as to be nearly irresistible.[3]

[1] See Stanmore, *Sidney Herbert*, vol. ii, ch. vi ; ed. Guedalla, *Gladstone and Palmerston*, pp. 56–8 and 113–18, 122–4, 146, 148 ; J. P. Baxter, *The Introduction of the Ironclad Warship* (Cambridge, Mass., 1933), chs. vii–viii
[2] Morley, *Gladstone*, vol. ii, p. 30, quoting *E.H.R.* (1887), p. 201
[3] See in general Morley, *Gladstone*, vol. ii, chs. i–iii

II

Only by taking into account this movement and the Cabinet struggle can English foreign policy during 1860 be explained. The least tractable problem is presented by Palmerston and Russell. For neither of them personally disapproved of the annexation of Savoy in itself, although both fulminated against it at the end of March. They had known of Napoleon's wish for Savoy from the first, and they knew Savoy was not much prized by Piedmont. Palmerston had not discouraged Persigny in December even when he suggested that England should actually propose the cession. On 5 February, however, Palmerston wrote to Russell, referring to inquiries made through Cowley in the previous month :

> The answer about Savoy is unsatisfactory, as you say ; the Emperor evidently means to have it. He will make a great mistake. He will destroy all Confidence in his Intentions of future Policy all over Europe ; . . . as regards England he will mar all the good effect upon Public Feeling and opinion which the Commercial Treaty . . . might have produced.[1]

But Palmerston still thought the annexation was a small price to pay for the regeneration of Italy. Announcing Gladstone's refusal to allow for the fortifications scheme in the Budget, the Prime Minister reverted at once to the Savoy Question : ' as far as England is concerned it would do little Harm for it would make People here more ready to complete our Defences.'[2] Russell, likewise, had grounded his complaints to Cowley and Hudson at the end of January less on the iniquity of the proposal itself than on the difficulties it would create for the English Government. He hoped Napoleon

[1] RP PRO 30/22/21   [2] 7 February, to Russell (RP PRO 30/22/21)

would sympathise : 'That scheme may surely be cast aside
to give confidence to Germany and England. I should expect
the Commercial Treaty, which is already not very popular,
to fail entirely in face of a proposed or announced annexation
of Savoy.' 'Our position here will be seriously damaged, and
Austria will rally all Germany to her side if such a beginning
of natural frontiers is made.' However, he believed that 'If
the King [of Sardinia] sells his inheritance of Savoy to obtain
Tuscany, he will be disgraced in the eyes of Europe, and we
shall not hesitate to affix to his conduct the fitting epithets.' [1]
But Russell gaily implied to the Queen that, even if Savoy
had to be sacrificed, 'well-wishers to mankind' must rejoice
at 'the liberation of the Italian people from a foreign yoke'.[2]
He was reluctant during February to send dispatches on Savoy
strong enough to please the Queen and the Cabinet, although
his colleagues 'warned him that in this case public opinion
would be at least as critical as the Queen.' [3] Both statesmen,
then, hoped the annexation could be prevented ; but neither
of them condemned it, for himself, wholeheartedly ; while
they both hinted that, if it took place, they would have to
oppose it publicly. Otherwise, as Persigny and Azeglio feared,
there would be another Orsini crisis, with France again responsible for the fall of a favourable English Ministry.[4]

Whether they fully realised it or not, however, Palmerston
and Russell were continually advising Piedmont to adopt, of
the two alternatives which Napoleon offered her, that one
which, as Napoleon viewed the question, necessarily involved
the annexation of Savoy. When Thouvenel revived the
scheme for an independent Central Italian Kingdom in

[1] 31 January, to both Cowley and Hudson (ed. Gooch, *Later Correspondence
of Russell*, vol. ii, pp. 256–7)   [2] 9 February (*QVL* vol. iii, pp. 387–9)
[3] 11 February, Granville to the Prince Consort (*ibid.* vol. iii, pp. 389–90)
[4] *CC Ing.* vol. ii, part ii, p. 18. G. Pagés, ' The Annexation of Savoy . . .',
in ed. A. Coville and H. W. V. Temperley, *Studies in Anglo-French History*
(Cambridge, 1935), p. 93

February, he may have been making a compromise proposal on Savoy : France might have permitted so much, but not Piedmont's annexation of the whole of North and Central Italy, without insisting on any compensation. It was even accompanied by another offer of Anglo-French alliance, like that of early January.[1] But Palmerston and Russell rejected it out of hand. 'I have been reading [wrote Palmerston] Thouvenel's scheme of Italian arrangement. I have seldom seen so much Paradox, and gratuitous assertion offered as a substitute for argument.'[2] In mid-March, when the idea of Tuscan autonomy was again pressed by France on Piedmont, he called it 'treacherous advice' : 'complete amalgamation is the only Foundation of National Unity and of National Strength.'[3] Russell had first said he would give Piedmont no advice. But he counselled rejection on 27 February.[4]

Plainly the two Ministers originally hoped to persuade Napoleon to abandon his scheme for Savoy and Nice even if Piedmont annexed the Duchies. Then, when it was made known early in March that the cession had been agreed upon, they demanded and expected that the Emperor would maintain the neutralisation of the two parts of the ceded territory nearest the Lake of Geneva, Chablais and Faucigny, as laid down by international treaty. This was the only complaint possible against what purported to be the voluntary cession by Piedmont of what were indisputably her own provinces to cede as she pleased. But virtually the whole transaction was complete by the end of March ; and, despite long

[1] 17 February, 'Very secret' dispatch from Cowley (F.O. 27/1333)
[2] 20 and 22 February, Russell to Cowley (F.O. 27/1323) ; 19 February, Palmerston to Russell (RP PRO 30/22/21)
[3] 16 March, Palmerston to Russell (RP PRO 30/22/21)
[4] 20, 22 and 27 February, to Hudson (F.O. 67/253). On the meaning of the compromise proposal, see R. C. Binkley, *Realism and Nationalism, 1852–1871* (New York, 1935), pp. 214–16. Cf. A. J. Whyte, *The Political Life and Letters of Cavour, 1848–61* (Oxford, 1930), pp. 352–8, and ed. R. Ciampini, *Il '59 in Toscana* (Florence, 1958), pp. 380–95

negotiations about a Congress to safeguard the rights of Switzerland, France was eventually left in complete control of the ceded area.

Palmerston and Russell had some ground for thinking they had been cheated. France and Piedmont had both at various times given apparently unambiguous undertakings not to make the objectionable arrangement.[1] Moreover, the manner of England's discomfiture was peculiarly galling. Napoleon's speech had been followed by the publication on 2 March of a dispatch from Thouvenel to Persigny, in which he claimed that France had been compelled to settle the Italian Question by herself because England had shown herself determined only to meddle and not to take any risks. Clarendon told Cowley :

People here are disposed to think that England has never received such a slap in the face as the Emperor's Speech and Thouvenel's despatch which was published immediately afterwards as if to make the speech more stinging, and yet there was nothing untrue in Thouvenel's despatch or that we did not deserve for thwarting the Emperor and . . . taking to ourselves credit for the arrangements agreeable to the Italians without our having made the smallest sacrifice or even being prepared to share with the Emperor the slightest responsibility.[2]

Furthermore, by making the cession dependent on a plebiscite, Cavour put it on exactly the same footing as the Duchies' annexation.

The English Ministers countered with a series of calculated indiscretions. Russell surprised the House of Commons on 26 March with a violent attack on France. He admitted that war for Savoy was impossible. But :

[1] See Pagés in ed. Coville and Temperley, *Studies in Anglo-French History*, pp. 96–7. And, e.g., *CC Ing.* vol. ii, part ii, p. 43
[2] 7 March (Wellesley, *The Paris Embassy*, pp. 198–9). 24 February, Thouvenel to Persigny, published in the *Moniteur* of 2 March

My opinion as I declared it in July and January I have no objection now to repeat—that such an act as the annexation of Savoy is one that will lead a nation so warlike as the French to call upon its Government from time to time to commit other acts of aggression ; and, therefore, I do feel that, however we may wish to live on the most friendly terms with the French Government, and certainly I do wish to live on the most friendly terms with that Government —we ought not to keep ourselves apart from the other nations of Europe, but that, when future questions may arise . . . we should be ready to act with others. . . .[1]

On the following day, Palmerston—who also acknowledged, privately, that war on this issue was unthinkable—assured the Comte de Flahaut, who was about to leave London and would soon see the Emperor, that Russell's speech expressed the unanimous feeling in England about French designs. He said he had lost all confidence in the Emperor and did not exclude the possibility of war with France. He made similar remarks to Azeglio and Persigny.[2]

Russell told Cowley that his object had been to save Chablais and Faucigny :

I certainly did not intend by my speech to please the French Govt. But I did not wish to repeat the operation of ' drifting into war ' ; so I determined to cast anchor.

What I mean is that the choler of the British nation, high, middle & low was rapidly rising, & if the Emperor had taken upon himself some day to discover that the people on the Rhine or in Belgium were panting to be annex'd to France we should have had such a burst here, as it would have been very difficult to curb.[3]

This was the crisis that Gladstone had feared, to guard against which was one of his objects in preparing his Budget :

---

[1] Quoted in Temperley & Penson, *Foundations of British Policy*, p. 211
[2] Ashley, *Palmerston*, vol. ii, pp. 190–2. *CC Ing.* vol. ii, part ii, pp. 59 and 61–2   [3] 26 and 31 March, Russell to Cowley (CP F.O. 519/197)

It should have been plain to all those who desired an united Italy, that such an Italy ought not to draw Savoy in its wake. . . . But it does not follow that Savoy should have been tacked on to France, while for the annexation of Nice it was difficult to find a word of apology. But it could scarcely be said to concern our interests, while there was not the shadow of a case of honour. The susceptibilities of England were, however, violently aroused. Even Lord Russell used imprudent language in parliament about looking for other allies. A French panic prevailed as strong as any of the other panics that have done so much discredit to this country. For this panic, the treaty of commerce was the only sedative. It was in fact a counter-irritant ; and it aroused the sense of commercial interest to counteract the war passion. It was and is my opinion, that the choice lay between the Cobden treaty and not the certainty, but the high probability, of a war with France.

In another account he spoke of ' a real risk of war against France, and possibly also against Italy '.[1] Clarendon saw the matter in a similar light from another angle—' England growling, but occupied in gnawing the Treaty Bone that has been flung at her '.[2] Gladstone may have been right in thinking that, if the cession had occurred without any previous attempt to mollify Anglo-French relations, it might well have brought the two Powers to war. For, as it was, it was enough to destroy almost all that remained of the old alliance.

New alliances were already under consideration. Early in the year, indeed, Russell had contemptuously rebuffed a suggestion by Prussia that there should be communications about French designs[3] ; on 13 February the Queen had proposed, but the Cabinet prevented, a circular dispatch on Savoy ; and the Cabinet had also declined to seem to threaten France by

[1] Morley, *Gladstone*, vol. ii, pp. 22–3, and Gladstone, *E.H.R.* (1887), p. 302
[2] 7 March, to Cowley (Wellesley, *The Paris Embassy*, p. 198), and *The Greville Memoirs*, vol. viii, p. 295
[3] Bell, *Palmerston*, vol. ii, p. 251. RA J. 23/50 and 52

consultations with other Powers.[1] But on 10 March it permitted exploratory dispatches inquiring the attitude of Austria, Russia and Prussia. Ten days later the Queen intervened again, strongly advocating united action to contain France—but to no avail.[2] Then on 28 March the Cabinet was asked to agree to Russell's summoning the London representatives of the Powers together at the Foreign Office. Again, though Palmerston supported some such consultation, the Cabinet demurred : Russell must see the envoys separately. The Queen expressed her *great* regret : the Emperor, ' who is playing a desperate game will [not] leave *time unemployed.*' [3] Next, the idea of a Conference of Foreign Ministers was rejected in favour of simply sending letters asking their opinions. The Queen ' signalised' the Cabinet's reluctance to make a coalition against France as a ' great error '.[4] To this point, she was almost alone in her desire to concert action against France. In fact Palmerston and Russell still seemed anxious to assist Napoleon when possible. Early in April Palmerston had to be prevented from expressing confidence in the Emperor in the House of Commons, which Persigny had asked him to do in order to counteract the effect of Russell's speech.[5]

Through April and May the dispute continued, but with Palmerston and Russell more and more taking the Queen's part. She would not hear of permitting England to negotiate

[1] The Queen to Russell and Palmerston (RA J. 26/47 and 48). Russell to the Queen (RF PRO 30/22/14). 18 February, Wood to the Prince Consort (RA J. 26/60)

[2] 10 March, Palmerston to the Queen (RA A. 28/40). Martin, *Life of the Prince Consort,* vol. v, p. 59. 20 March, the Queen to Russell (RA J. 27/59)

[3] 27 March, the Queen to Russell and Russell to the Queen (RA J. 27/107 and 108). 29 March, Russell to the Queen and the Queen to Russell (RA J. 27/117 and 118)

[4] 20 March, Palmerston to the Queen (RA J. 27/125) ; Albert's introduction to RA J. 27

[5] 1 April, Palmerston to Russell (RP PRO 30/22/21). 2 April, Russell to the Queen and the Queen to Russell (RA J. 27/133 and 134, the latter in *QVL* vol. iii, pp. 395-6)

by herself with France over Savoy, which the Cabinet hoped might be successful: that was Napoleon's game. Unfortunately, however, there seemed no more satisfactory alternative: the request made to Austria, Prussia and Russia for their opinions on the Savoy Question produced a satisfactory answer only from Prussia. For Russia was France's ally; and Austria, having ceded Lombardy amid English expressions of delight, thought the indignation over Savoy excessive. But on 21 April, as Granville reported to the Prince:

Lord John stated [to the Cabinet] the substance of a secret despatch from Ct Rechberg to Count Apponyi, as suggesting an agreement between the two great German Powers & Her Majesty, to resist future encroachments of France, and practically embracing a guarantee from us of Venetia, & even of the Bourbons at Naples. . . . He said that it was impossible to give any guarantee but he proposed to enter into an Agreement with Austria and Prussia that we should all communicate when any such events arose. He was supported by Lord Palmerston, but Sir G. Grey, Sir G. Lewis, Mr. Gladstone, Sir Charles Wood, the Chancellor and indeed all the Cabinet objected. They said that such a treaty would be known, would be considered a treaty of alliance, that it would irritate the French *Nation*, & would consolidate the alliance between France & Russia, while it would bind Austria & Prussia to nothing. Some hinted that having declined a warlike alliance with France, they did not wish to enter into a warlike alliance against her.

Granville suggested reserving England's position, only Palmerston now opposing. But, as Granville concluded, ' I am afraid Your Royal Highness will be with Lord Palmerston.'[1] The Queen returned to the charge on 5 May, alarmed by one of the many rumours of French plots, this time a supposed overture to Austria that Venetia would be guaranteed if Napoleon could take the left bank of the Rhine:

[1] RA J. 28/38

If this is *allowed* to go on, bloody wars and universal misery must be the consequences. There exists in the Queen's opinion but one means of arresting this, and that is an *intimate and avowed* union between the European Powers, who should agree not to enter separately into engagements with France, but at once to communicate to each other what comes from France and preconcert their steps together. . . . Such an alliance would not be based upon an agreement to go to war together in a future and hypothetical case, but rather to act in concert and honest friendship together diplomatically *in the present*, in order to prevent the Emperor bringing Europe to that condition in which war will become a necessity.

On the same day Gladstone wrote : ' Three wild schemes of alliance are afloat ! Our old men (2) are unhappily our youngest.'[1] Presumably he was referring to variants of these royal proposals, with perhaps also some plan for interference in Italy, since Hudson was making frequent suggestions for Anglo-French intervention in Naples and Sicily.[2] A week later Russell reported to the Queen that the Cabinet had again declined to permit more than non-committal communications with other Powers. The Queen replied with a Memorandum, advising, as ' the most simple & least dangerous step the Q. can think of ', ' a union with the German Powers, having for its object to watch France '. If the Cabinet still rejected the advice, she demanded a formal Minute taking all responsibility off her shoulders for the disasters that would ensue.[3] Palmerston at first seems to have agreed with her ; and, though Russell thought her too ready to quarrel with France, the Cabinet commissioned the Prime Minister to draft

[1] RP PRO 30/22/66, esp. 1 May, to Russell
[2] RA J. 28/82, in ed. Gooch, *Later Correspondence of Russell*, p. 259. Morley, *Gladstone*, vol. ii, p. 31
[3] 12 May, Russell to the Queen (RA J. 28/99). 13 May, the Queen's Memorandum in RP PRO 30/22/14. Also RA J. 28/107

a Minute.[1] But by the end of the month it was clear that
the Cabinet would certainly go no further than allow the
sort of exploratory communications which Russell had already
begun. The Foreign Secretary himself preferred a course
' between the general coalition recommended by the Queen,
& a special alliance with France on which we can no longer
place reliance '.[2] The Cabinet refused to adopt Palmerston's
Minute, which, after much abuse of France, proposed ' diplomatic action backed by known strength ', and which the
Prince considered ' excellent '; the Ministers decided that
there was too much unsubstantiated criticism of France, and
that in any case Cabinet Minutes were to be kept for very
special occasions. On this occasion a combination of the
Queen and the Prime Minister had been defeated by the
Cabinet.[3] As Palmerston informed her on 9 June, the Cabinet
was unwilling to be committed to anything.[4]

Napoleon's deceptions over Savoy appeared to have
alienated Palmerston almost completely. But it is notice-
able that his more violent condemnations of the Emperor
were made to those most likely to be impressed or pleased
by them—the French and Piedmontese envoys, and the
Queen and Prince.[5] His outlook had not changed so radically from his ambivalent attitude of the previous year :
that Napoleon had dangerous designs, but that England's
position compelled her to act with him, and that she must
hope thereby to curb them. He cannot have been altogether
surprised by the manner of the annexation, and he certainly

[1] 14 May, Russell to Palmerston (BMS). 16 May, Russell to the Queen
(RA J. 28/116) and 17 May, Palmerston to the Queen (RA A. 28/75)
[2] 28 May, to Palmerston (BMS)
[3] Draft Minute in RA J. 28/143. Albert's Introduction to vol. J.29.
2 June, Palmerston to the Queen (RA J. 29/15)   [4] RA J. 29/30
[5] Azeglio was, I think, deceived in saying : ' Ce n'est certainement pas
moi que le [sic] hommes d'Etat de ce pays prennent pour confident de leurs
méfiances contre vous ' (CC Ing. vol. ii, part ii, p. 65, 14 April, to Cavour).

could not claim to have consistently opposed it. He presumably felt somewhat affronted by the Emperor's treatment of him. But, despite all the *bravura*, it seems plausible to contend that he in fact kept a level head, shifting the emphasis of his policy to suit the new circumstances, in which a close alliance with France was out of the question. He had always feared French expansionist schemes : he saw dangers to Gibraltar in 1859 just as he was to be alarmed by France 'partant pour la Syrie' in 1860.[1] He had always believed that England's armaments preparations would tend to deter France from further attempts at aggrandisement. He now stressed the point more, because the alliance control had become impracticable. But he did not rule out the possibility, even now, of using her. His attitude had altered, but this was not a *volte-face*. Nor was the change due to personal pique, but public necessity.

Gladstone now headed the opposite party in the Cabinet on this, the principal issue of foreign policy, as well as on most internal matters. He had been convinced by Napoleon's amenability during the Commercial Treaty negotiations that his good faith could in general be assumed. His extraordinary remark in January, that 'I really desire no more than to live in the same boat with him, a stoker or sub-stoker on his engine', showed how far he had then gone towards trusting him implicitly ; and his recognition of Napoleon's efforts on behalf of Free Trade and Italy kept him sympathetic throughout 1860. In September, to use his own curious distinction, he did not incline to 'place reliance on the French Emperor'; but rather to 'interpret him candidly'. He did not believe that the arming of England would deter the Emperor ; he thought it was likely to bring war nearer.[2]

[1] Bell, *Palmerston*, vol. ii, p. 269
[2] 16 September, to Lacaita (Morley, *Gladstone*, vol. ii, p. 15). 18 January, to Brougham (GP BM Add MS 44530, f.146). Morley, *Gladstone*, vol. ii, ch. iii

Other Ministers were less extreme. The difrence between the two chiefs—for Russell usually followed Pamerston—and the bulk of the Cabinet on foreign policy was basically that between the ' most combative ' and the ' least combative ', the advocates of an active foreign policy *versus* the non-interventionists.[1] Between the Court and the Cabinet majority, of course, there was a much wider gulf. As Clarenon wrote to Cowley on 7 July, the Prince ' is so violent about The Empr. that it is hard to understand what policy he wd. wish to see pursued.' Sometimes, Clarendon even wonderd if the Court wanted peace with France. The Prince was almost ' demented ' and ' he won't see the difference betwen that intimate confidential alliance which existed four years ago and is now impossible, and keeping on such good and watchful terms with the Emperor as might serve to restrain him from perpetrating the crimes that are feared and that he may meditate.' [2] But the Cabinet always succeeded in imposing moderation, whether or not Palmerston and Russell supported the Queen and the Prince.

III

No sooner had Hudson written to Russell trying to excuse the cession of Savoy and Nice than he was able to turn to more congenial news. On 25 March he announced : ' Since I wrote to you yesterday the Italian question has made another stride in advance. The Sicilians are demanding annexation to Sardinia.' [3] The revolt was on the point of extinction when Garibaldi sailed from Genoa early in May to its aid. He revived it, and from the moment of his landing until

[1] *ibid.* vol. ii, p. 635
[2] CP F.O. 519/178 (partly quoted in Wellesley, *The Paris Embassy*, p. 207)
[3] RP PRO 30/22/66

the beginning of October, when he fought a drawn battle on the Volturno north of Naples, his success was almost uninterrupted: he took Palermo on 27 May; he won a battle at Milazzo on 20 July; he crossed the Straits of Messina on 18–19 August; and he entered Naples on 7 September. At the end of May unification became an accepted possibility; before the end of July it was a probability.

On two points England's position was quite clear. Despite the suspicions of many contemporaries and some modern historians, there is no evidence that any English statesman had any idea of annexing Sicily. The Conservative Government had solemnly repudiated the notion in May 1859, and Russell never mentioned it except to discountenance it.[1] Second, there was no possibility that England would support the King of Naples unless and until he reformed his system of government. For years she had been urging him to restore the 1848 Constitution on the mainland and the 1812 Constitution in Sicily; and some such change was always made a precondition of any English aid. In case there should be any doubt about England's views on the régime, Palmerston and Russell frequently expounded them to Neapolitan envoys. Palmerston drove Targioni to ask for his recall by assuring him at a Drawing Room that the universe would rejoice at the fall of the dynasty ! Ludolf was told that he represented a Government worse than the Hessians' or the Turks'.[2] And Russell, when asked to help the King, said good care would be taken to do nothing of the kind.[3] On this subject the opinions of the Prime Minister and the Foreign Secretary, though excep-

[1] 1 May 1859, Malmesbury to Crampton, quoted in Temperley & Penson, *Foundations of British Foreign Policy*, p. 202. 15 and 22 May 1860, Russell to Cowley (CP F.O. 519/197)

[2] *CC Ing.* vol. ii, part ii, pp. 60, 69. cf. *The Greville Memoirs*, vol. viii, pp. 309–10

[3] 1 June, Azeglio to Cavour (*CC Ing.* vol. ii, part ii, p. 73)

tionally strong, were not in substance different from those of
their Cabinet colleagues.

There was great uncertainty, however, what, from England's
point of view, would be the best arrangement in South Italy.
It was generally held that it was to the interest of England that
the peninsula should be politically divided into two parts.
Palmerston thought so ' because a separate kingdom of the
Two Sicilies would be more likely, in the event of war between
England and France, to side, at least by its neutrality, with
the strongest Naval Power, and it is to be hoped that such
Power would be England '.[1] Cowley agreed with him, and
so at first did Russell and Hudson.[2] In the early weeks of
Garibaldi's expedition, only the fate of Sicily was in question ;
and the English experts then favoured independence for the
island.[3] But Palmerston already thought that there would be
' no strong objection to the union of all Italy and of the
Island of Sicily into one Monarchy ' [4] ; and Henry Elliot,
the Minister in Naples, took the same view.[5]

So England was decidedly in favour of change, and was
not unwilling to accept any of the possible outcomes of a loca-
lised conflict between Garibaldi and the Neapolitan dynasty.
She was already committed to non-intervention in internal
Italian affairs ; and, though Russell, like Gladstone, believed
that it would be morally justifiable to intervene against the
old régime, he thought it would be inexpedient.[6]

What made Palmerston and Russell sometimes consider
taking action was the recurring possibility that other Powers

[1] 10 January 1861, to the Queen (*QVL* vol. iii, p. 428)
[2] 6 December 1860, Cowley to Clarendon (Maxwell, *Clarendon*, vol. ii,
p. 231). 16 June, Russell to Cowley (CP F.O. 519/197). 18 May, Hudson
to Russell (RP PRO 30/22/66), quoted in G. M. Trevelyan, *Garibaldi and the
Making of Italy* (London, 1912), p. 306
[3] 29 May, Elliot to Russell (RP PRO 30/22/85). 28 May, Palmerston to
Russell (BMS)   [4] 17 May, to Russell (RP PRO 30/22/21)
[5] 29 May, to Russell (RP PRO 30/22/85)
[6] 1 May, Russell to the Queen (RA J. 28/66)

might intervene. On 6 June the Foreign Secretary told
Azeglio, without Cabinet authority, that England would
oppose Austria if she interfered.[1] France, however, was the
real bogy. No one knew how far Garibaldi was backed
by and obedient to Cavour, nor what understanding there
might be between France and Piedmont. The English statesmen now distrusted Cavour, for his behaviour over Savoy.
Russell wrote on 1 May : ' I am happy to think Cavour is
likely to fall. He is too French, & too tricky.' [2] In late
June he called him ' little more than a Prefect of the Depart-
ment of the Po '. [3] Soon after the cession of Savoy and Nice,
Azeglio had described the English outlook very well, fresh
from one of his intimate conversations with Palmerston :

The moral effect of these cessions, like the stain of the partition of
Poland, will never be erased in England. Only great and glorious
advances towards the reawakening of Italy will neutralise the
impression they have made. . . . An essential distinction must be
kept in view. The English and their present Ministers criticise
certain men who are in the forefront of Italian politics. But at
the same time, Italy is still for them what it was before, a favoured
land whose progress and education they watch with the liveliest
sympathies. They take the same interest as formerly in the march
of events, wishing for nothing better than to see us annex the
whole peninsula. They merely say to us : If you are achieving
these results purely by internal revolutions, go ahead. But if, to
round off your territory, you must turn the universe upside down
to fish in troubled waters, and if, to obtain Venetia, Umbria, etc.,
you must plot with France to extend her as far as her natural
frontiers and to cause confusion in the East, then you must stop,
for it is no longer Italy which is at stake but the peace and balance
of all Europe.[4]

[1] 6 June, Azeglio to Cavour (*CC Ing.* vol. ii, part ii, p. 76)
[2] To Palmerston (BMS)
[3] 25 June, to Hudson (RP PRO 30/22/109)
[4] 14 April, to Cavour (*CC Ing.* vol. ii, part ii, pp. 65–6)

Palmerston and Russell seem to have been inclined to believe the rumours that Napoleon intended to demand Genoa or the island of Sardinia. Certainly they did not propose to be caught napping a second time.

Palmerston's remedy was an alliance with Piedmont to sustain her against French pressure. On 17 May he wrote :

We ought without Delay to come to a definite understanding, and a distinct engagement with Sardinia about Italian affairs. No Body can doubt that Garibaldis Expedition has been planned encouraged and assisted by the Government of Turin. . . .

[We should tell Sardinia an alliance with Great Britain could alone assure us that she intended no cession of territory], and that a Refusal to conclude such a Treaty will be deemed by the British Govt as an indirect admission of the Truth of the Rumours. . . .

If such a Treaty is signed we should withdraw & stand aloof from the Sicilian and Neapolitan Insurrection ; if the Treaty is declined we should tell the King of Naples that our desire is to maintain his Dynasty and the Integrity of his Dominions, but that we cannot be of any active assistance to him unless he will at once alter his System of Government . . . ; That if he will do this and immediately we will endeavour by our Naval Force to prevent all landings of hostile Bands in any Part of his Dominions, and give him moreover our political support.[1]

Russell could not 'stomach defending Bombino'. 'Nor would the country.' But he thought Piedmont might be guaranteed against French demands on condition that she promised not to attack Venetia. 'It seems to me that we ought as much as possible to have the feeling of Italian independence in our favour.'[2] As usual, the Cabinet, when consulted, proved less adventurous than the two elder

[1] To Russell (RP PRO 30/22/21)
[2] 18 May, Russell to Palmerston (RP PRO 30/22/30 and ed. Gooch, *Later Correspondence of Russell*, vol. ii, p. 260, where, if he used the same version, the editor failed to mark omissions and modified the wording).

statesmen ; and the resulting dispatch of 22 May merely asked Cavour to refrain from further cessions. The Queen lamented the Cabinet's weakness.[1] It was without the backing of his colleagues that Russell on 6 June angled for a request from Piedmont for an alliance.[2]

At long last, on 25 June, the young King of Naples granted Home Rule to Sicily, restored the Neapolitan Constitution of 1848, and sued for an alliance with Piedmont—the programme for his salvation recommended by France, who also proposed a truce between Garibaldi and the King. England could not but feel some compulsion to take the part of a Government which had, albeit in extremity, accepted her advice. So, during the crucial month of July, her diplomacy was hesitant and confused, torn between diffident support for Naples, timid approbation of Garibaldi, and suspicious fear of France.

In particular, Palmerston and Russell gave much and various advice to Piedmont, to the Sicilians and to Garibaldi. The last had declared for the annexation of Sicily to Piedmont, but he did not wish to effect it until he had conquered Naples as well. The Prime Minister and the Foreign Secretary most commonly counselled immediate annexation, which Cavour at this stage seemed to desire, and which seemed the safest solution since it would probably entail Garibaldi's abandoning the invasion of the mainland. They expressed this opinion in private conversations with Panizzi, Azeglio and the Sicilian envoy ; and they had private letters sent to Garibaldi in the same sense,

---

[1] *Further Correspondence . . . Italy* (State Papers. Session 5 February–6 August, 1861. Vol. lxvii. Command Paper No. 2757) [from this point referred to as *Further Correspondence*], p. 125. 24 May, the Queen to Russell (RP PRO 30/22/14)

[2] 6 June Azeglio to Cavour (*CC Ing.* vol. ii, part ii, p. 78). I can find no evidence for the statement of Mr A. J. P. Taylor (*Struggle for Mastery in Europe*, pp. 120–1) that ' The British Government . . . offered Cavour a defensive alliance '.

and urging him to conclude a truce with the Neapolitan
Government. They usually added, however, that Sicily must
have full freedom to choose or reject annexation.[1] At other
times they recommended the continued union of Naples and
Sicily separate from the rest of Italy, both as an English interest
and as perhaps the best guarantee against French claims for
compensation, and because they feared that Piedmont would
not be able to govern all Italy efficiently.[2] Stating this preference involved answering the difficult questions, who could
be found to rule the Two Sicilies and how was he to be
installed. An independent Sicily was still sometimes contemplated, but this enhanced the dynastic problem.[3] In fact they
hardly knew what they wanted. Russell sometimes abstained
altogether from giving an opinion ; and even Palmerston once
prefaced some detailed advice with the confession, that, 'if . . .
omnipotence were magically conferred upon him, he would
not really know what to decide, or, to begin with, what to
aim at '.[4]

Azeglio had the key to these shifts of policy : ' Evidently ',
he reported on 22 July, ' England ceased to press for the unification of Italy from the moment when she thought she was working thereby for the aggrandisement of France.' Palmerston
and Russell had stopped advising annexation when they heard
of an alleged secret treaty ceding Genoa, Sardinia and Elba to
France.[5] Such prospects were widely credited. Elliot said that
' except Hudson [who by now was advocating unification],
there are few people in their senses who believe that France
would consent to an united Italy without exacting at least an

[1] 16 July, Azeglio to Cavour (CC Ing. vol. ii, part ii, pp. 98–100). 23 July,
Russell to Hudson (RP PRO 30/22/111)
[2] 22 and 26 July, Azeglio to Cavour (CC Ing. vol. ii, part ii, pp. 103–04, 113)
[3] See ibid. vol. ii, part ii, pp. 110, 112, 113 ; and Palmerston-Russell
correspondence in RP PRO 30/22/21
[4] 16 and 26 July, Azeglio to Cavour (CC Ing. vol. ii, part ii, pp. 98, 113)
[5] 22 July, to Cavour (ibid. vol. ii, part ii, pp. 103–04)

equivalent.'[1] Hence on 10 July Palmerston had revived his
scheme of May for a Piedmontese alliance against France, with
a guarantee of Naples if Cavour should refuse. But Russell
had thought ' on the whole we shall do better by not making
any positive proposal to Sardinia. Her conduct is equivocal,
& I fear we cannot make it straightforward.'[2] There was as
yet no likelihood of English intervention. But a serious threat
of French aggrandisement might have brought it near.

England's official statements were more consistent and less
numerous than the private remarks of Palmerston and Russell.
The Queen endeavoured to prevent the Government committing itself to any particular scheme for South Italy [3] ; and the
Cabinet could be relied upon to reject proposals for positive
action. Between 23 and 26 July, however, a policy was
embodied in dispatches. To Cowley on the 23rd Russell
wrote that England would not approve any new territorial
acquisitions by France ; that she did not wish for the unification of Italy ; but that, if the attempts to ' conciliate ' the
pretensions of Piedmont and Naples in Sicily failed, then
perhaps Italy might after all be united ; and that England
and France should leave the inhabitants of South Italy to
decide their own fate. To Hudson on 25 July Russell recommended the alliance between Piedmont and Naples. And on
26 July, to Cowley again, he announced that the Cabinet had
rejected a French proposal of armed mediation in the Straits
of Messina.[4]

One misunderstanding must be righted, concerning ' the
Lacaita incident '. Dr Trevelyan, in his classic account
of Garibaldi's expedition, described how Lacaita, by calling

---

[1] 10 July, to Russell (RP PRO 30/22/85)
[2] 10 July, Palmerston to Russell (RP PRO 30/22/21). 14 July, Russell to
Palmerston (BMS)
[3] esp. 14 July, to Russell (RA J. 29/98)
[4] *Further Correspondence*, pp. 143-8

on Russell at a decisive moment on 24 July, believed himself
to have averted English intervention against the hero.[1] Lacaita
alleged that he had been commissioned by Cavour to forestall
this step. The facts are these. Cavour on 23 and 24 July sent
obscurely worded telegrams to Azeglio, from which the envoy
gathered that Cavour wished him to arrange, through unofficial
channels, that England should oppose the truce between
Garibaldi and Naples, advocated by France and publicly supported by Piedmont. As well as the truce, France had proposed Anglo-French mediation ; and Persigny in London was
claiming that England was ready to agree. So Azeglio sent
all his ' spies '—Panizzi, Lacaita, Shaftesbury and the Sicilian
representative—to find out the attitudes of Palmerston and
Russell. They learned that, at an interview with the Neapolitan
envoy, ' Lord John had already rejected mediation because, if
it failed, the discomfited mediators would escape ridicule only
if they showed their claws and thereby infringed the principle
of non-intervention.' On the other hand, as has been seen,
England had already advised the truce.[2] Russell in fact had
never favoured armed mediation. He had told the Queen on
23 July that ' The only hope which the King of Naples can
entertain must rest on the fidelity of his army & navy in
defending the Neapolitan territory.'[3] And he wrote to
Cowley on 24 July : ' It seems there is an itching desire for
armed intervention between Naples and Sicily. But I shall
lend no ear to it.'[4] The only evidence that Russell had
agreed to it was the impression of Persigny to that effect.
The French Ambassador was well known both for imagina-
tiveness and for a tendency to browbeat. He had surprised
the Foreign Secretary with the statement that Palmerston

[1] *Garibaldi and the Making of Italy*, pp. 103–09
[2] 26 July, Azeglio to Cavour (*CC Ing.* vol. ii, part ii, pp. 110–14)
[3] RA J. 29/115   [4] CP F.O. 519/197

approved armed mediation ; Russell was at this moment estranged from Palmerston ; and so he temporised, saying that the Cabinet must settle the matter the next day. It subsequently emerged that Persigny's description of Palmerston's view had been quite misleading : Palmerston had no intention of joining with France or interfering in Sicily. The cause of the temporary coolness between the two Ministers was a disagreement over policy in Syria : Russell was willing, and Palmerston was not, to join the Emperor in sending an expedition there. On that question the Cabinet of 25 July did overrule Russell. But on Italy it took his advice. ' The Lacaita incident ', in fact, was of no great importance ; Lacaita in after years allowed his memory to exaggerate what he had done in the cause of unification.[1]

The English Government had positively declined to interfere in South Italy. Napoleon now did the same, in a letter of 25 July to Persigny, designed for publication. He also disclaimed any idea of asking compensation for Piedmontese aggrandisement.[2] He kept his word, except that he intervened to protect the King of Naples in his last stronghold of Gaeta at the end of October, when unification had been virtually completed. Thus the Emperor had given up his plan of mediation, despite the fact that England had specifically allowed him to proceed under pain only of a protest.[3] France was again conniving at her own exclusion from the Italian peninsula.

From this point Italian affairs went on ' at Railway Speed '[4] ; and the English Ministers, for the most part, allowed events to take their course. Russell was in Scotland for the bulk of

---

[1] See the admirable article by M. Avetta, ' Studi Cavouriani I : Una " vexata quaestio " alla luce dei carteggi cavouriani ', *Rass. stor. del Ris.*, vol. xxi (1) (1934), pp. 49–71

[2] Printed in Maxwell, *Clarendon*, vol. ii, pp. 217–19

[3] 26 July, Russell to Cowley (*Further Correspondence*, pp. 147–8)

[4] 28 September, Palmerston to Russell (RP PRO 30/22/21)

September, and then in Coburg until mid-October. The Cabinet dispersed thankfully, late in August, at the end of the very long Parliamentary session ; it did not meet again until 20 October ; then it adjourned until 13 November.[1] During this period some unofficial pressure was put on Garibaldi to prevent his advancing on Rome,[2] and Palmerston commended Cavour's invasion of Umbria and the Marches.[3] But England made no official statement about it till the end of October. It is necessary to consider in detail only four incidents of this last phase, which are of special interest for the formation of policy.

On 31 August, from Scotland, the Foreign Secretary warned Piedmont in a dispatch that England had interests in the Adriatic which she must carefully watch. Palmerston had objected to this document, and the Cabinet did not see it. Only the Queen approved.[4] When Cavour published it, Russell was taken to task by the Cabinet. Azeglio reported :

Panizzi . . . dined with the Duke of Somerset and Gladstone. Both talked in the sense most favourable for our affairs and spoke with great energy against Lord John's Note which they stigmatised as ' Holy Alliance Style '. They fully confirmed . . . that Lord John wrote without consulting his colleagues who intend on his return to have it out with him.

Gladstone was even more expansive : he did not contest that there had been attempts to drag the country into imprudent alliances. But, he added, as long as the present Government exists, that will not happen, or at least not without a group leaving the Cabinet. He then let it be understood what his words meant, by adding that certain people had reached the

[1] RA J. 30 and A. 28/152
[2] Trevelyan, *Garibaldi and the Making of Italy*, p. 190
[3] 19 September, Azeglio to Cavour (*CC Ing.* vol. ii, part ii, p. 125)
[4] *Further Correspondence*, pp. 157-8. 30 August, Russell to the Queen (RA J. 30/54). 9 October, Azeglio to Cavour (*CC Ing.* vol. ii, part ii, p. 140)

stage of wanting to make English policy the antechamber of Prussia's.[1]

To make up for this misdemeanour, Russell sent on 27 October, with Palmerston's approval, but without Cabinet consultation, a sensational dispatch, in the nature of a proclamation, rejoicing at 'the gratifying prospect of a people building up the edifice of their liberties, and consolidating the work of their independence, amid the sympathies and good wishes of Europe'.[2] The Queen and Prince had allowed this dispatch to be sent because 'it was so much less bad than what they had been led to expect, and because they thought it would appear some months hence in a Blue Book and be comparatively unobserved.'[3] But it was quickly published. It justified the actions of Cavour and Garibaldi on general principles, and contradicted previous opinions that Italy was an exceptional case.[4] It was partly designed to deter the Sovereigns of Russia, Austria and Prussia, who were meeting in Warsaw, from any intervention they might be contemplating against Italy.

Spain was also supposed to be considering intervention. At first Palmerston wished to threaten that England would prevent her. But Russell did 'not believe in the Spanish Story at all', and thought it was a French trick to encourage a renewal of the alliance. However, 'if Austria or Spain, or any other Power attempts to interfere with Italy in her progress to re-construction I think we must stand by Italy. I would

---

[1] 15 October, to Cavour (*CC Ing.* vol. ii, part ii, pp. 142–3). cf. 29 October, Russell to Hudson (ed. Gooch, *Later Correspondence of Russell*, vol. ii, p. 267) : this letter cannot refer to the appearance of the dispatch of 27 October, which was delayed ; it was that of 31 August which 'Cavour has done me a good deal of harm by publishing.'

[2] To Hudson (Walpole, *Russell*, vol. ii, pp. 325–7)

[3] 24 November, Clarendon to Cowley (printed in part, undated, in Wellesley, *The Paris Embassy*, p. 213) (CP F.O. 519/178)

[4] e.g. 4 October, Russell to Crampton (*Further Correspondence*, p. 200)

rather do this without France, but that may be difficult.'[1] Russell then prepared a circular to discourage all the Powers from intervention, which he said he would be ready to send without consulting the Cabinet. But 'the Queen for one [was] not prepared to go to war to ensure the success of the Italian Revolution,' and she had the draft toned down. Besides vague menaces, it had expressed the hope that Rome and Venetia would soon achieve freedom. Even then, it still failed to get between the 'Scylla and Charybdis of Court and Cabinet'.[2]

Palmerston in December tried to induce the Cabinet to make suggestions to Austria to sell Venetia. It had long been his special desire that North Italy should be entirely free. Russell, however, was reluctant to make any recommendation, for it was still his opinion that Venice was the gate to Vienna. But he was eventually enlisted behind Palmerston. It appeared that war might break out again in the spring, and all indications pointed to Dalmatia and Hungary as the danger-spots, since Cavour and Napoleon were believed to be dabbling in the discontents of these Austrian provinces. Palmerston and Russell contended that, Venetia once ceded, Italy and Austria could be friendly, and then France would cease to influence the new Kingdom. A kind of guarantee of Dalmatia was proposed by Russell as the bribe to Austria.[3] Lewis took the lead in

---

[1] 26 and 29 October, Palmerston to Russell (RP PRO 30/22/21). 26 and 28 October, Russell to Palmerston (BMS)

[2] 30 October, Russell to Palmerston (BMS). 3 November, the Queen to Russell (*QVL* vol. iii, p. 411). 9, 11 and 12 November, Palmerston to Russell (RP PRO 30/22/21)

In Temperley and Penson, *Foundations of British Policy*, pp. 221, 226, the letter of Palmerston of 29 October is cited as 'definite proof that Palmerston warned off Spain from armed interference in Italy by a threat of force'. But it in fact shows, what the other documents in BMS show still more clearly, that, though Palmerston wished to do so, he was prevented. See F.O. 72/976

[3] 2 December, Russell to Palmerston (BMS). Bell, *Palmerston*, vol. ii, pp. 266–7

opposing the plan in Cabinet, though naturally with powerful support from the Court.[1] After a battle of the familiar type the Queen prevented any public allusion to the matter. As she pointed out, nothing could well be more tempting to Piedmont, and perhaps to France as her ally, than to take up the words of England as a justification for an invasion of Venetia.[2]

Both officially and unofficially, England's policy towards South Italy had been inconsistent. She had flaunted her detestation of the old Neapolitan system of Government, and had left no doubt that her neutrality was malevolent towards it. Admiral Mundy, commanding the squadron sent to protect British citizens, had protested, to no avail, against the bombardment of Palermo.[3] The home Government had echoed him.[4] England had usually upheld the principle of self-determination. But she had not wholeheartedly supported Garibaldi ; and her strongest expression of opinion before the end of October had been in favour of a dualist Italy. She had been, officially, more disturbed by fear of France than excited by the emancipation of Italy. The dispatch of 27 October was a rousing justification of an outcome which England had hitherto deprecated.

She had avoided active interference in South Italy. Her abstention was partly due to the confusion of the international situation : it was extremely difficult to predict the results of any course of action. The cession of Savoy and Nice had contributed also, since it had made impossible the only alliance

---

[1] 1 and 8 December, Lewis to Palmerston ; 1 December, Palmerston to Lewis (BMS)

[2] See RA vol. J. 31, esp. nos. 115 (15 December, Russell to the Queen) ; 117 (16 December, the Queen to Russell, printed in ed. Gooch, *Later Correspondence of Russell*, vol. ii, pp. 268–9) ; and 118 (16 December, Wood to General Grey)

[3] Trevelyan, *Garibaldi and the Thousand*, pp. 289–91, and *Garibaldi and the Making of Italy*, pp. 307–08   [4] 21 June, Russell to Elliot (F.O. 70/312)

which had seemed probable at the end of 1859, and since it had spread distrust of another potential ally, Piedmont. In terms of English politics, however, the saviour of non-intervention was the Cabinet. It is true that the Prime Minister and Foreign Secretary seem to have been accorded—or to have allowed themselves—more latitude than in 1859 in giving advice to other Powers in official dispatches. But, whenever it came to a proposal for action, the Cabinet had to be consulted, and always rejected it. What Gladstone called 'those strange sins of foreign policy' had generally been 'nipped in the bud à l'unanimité'.[1]

IV

In the early part of the year the Government had been conscious of, and had bowed to, very strong pressure from Parliament and the public on the Savoy Question. Russell had been forced by Parliament to lay papers which he would have preferred to withhold and which contained decidedly embarrassing information bearing on the Cabinet's complicity in Napoleon's design.[2] Eventually he had fallen in with the bitter feeling against France.

On purely Italian matters, however, Parliament was very tolerant. The Blue Book on the negotiations of 1859 caused no difficulty when it appeared in February 1860. On 12 July 1860 the Foreign Secretary gave the House of Commons a fair account of the Government's policy in Sicily, stressing its open mind and its wish for self-determination [3] ; but few M.P.s other than the Roman Catholics objected. At the

[1] 3 September, to Argyll (Morley, *Gladstone*, vol. ii, p. 637)
[2] *Parl. Deb.*, 3rd series, vol. clvi, cols. 262–3, 445–6, 1001–35, 1933–70, 2143 ; and vol. clvii, cols. 2112–40. See H. W. V. Temperley & L. M. Penson, *A Century of Diplomatic Blue Books, 1814–1914* (Cambridge, 1938), Preface and p. 163   [3] *Parl. Deb.*, 3rd series, vol. clviii, cols. 1876–95

last discussion of the session on foreign policy, on 24 August, the House was counted out.[1] The conquest of Naples occurred during the recess, and so the papers relating to the last phase of unification could not appear until 1861.

Russell himself was conscious of only two unpopular acts in the course of his South Italian policy, the support he gave to a truce between Garibaldi and the King of Naples, and the dispatch of 31 August.[2] Both of these actions he cancelled with his pronouncement of 27 October.

V

In the Liberal Cabinet the initiative in foreign policy came nearly always from Palmerston and Russell, although occasionally, as in the case of the projected German alliance, it came from the Queen. Of the two statesmen Russell has received more credit for the Government's Italian policy. Palmerston himself praised the Foreign Secretary highly. He wrote on 23 August 1859 that, if Russell succeeded in his latest proposal, he ' would have done more for Italy with [his] Pen, than Napoleon 3 has accomplished with his sword '.[3] Again, on 7 February 1860, Palmerston wrote : ' I am glad you see a clear Horizon about the Settlement of Italy ; if you succeed in making a respectable State out of Northern & Central Italy you will deserve to have your Statue erected at Arona and on the best bridge over the Arno.'[4] Hudson went even further. On 19 October 1860 he told the Foreign Secretary : ' I hope my dear Lord on the 23rd of this Month to congratulate you on the final welding of one of those great

[1] ibid. vol. clx, col. 1811
[2] 7 September, to Cowley (Further Correspondence, pp. 161–2). 29 October to Hudson (ed. Gooch, Later Correspondence of Russell, vol. ii, p. 267)
[3] RP PRO 30/22/20   [4] RP PRO 30/22/21

links in the chain of Liberty, intelligence and reason which
you placed on the Political Anvil when you laid the 1st Reform
Bill on the Table of the H. of Commons.'[1] The historian
should be on his guard against such eulogies. In fact it is
clear that Palmerston was the dominant figure, brilliantly
managing a difficult colleague. He corrected Russell's
dispatches, sometimes caustically. He composed at least one,
of great importance.[2] And, as Greville heard :

Palmerston has obtained an entire influence and authority over
Lord John, who only sees with his eyes and without any contest
submits to be entirely guided and controlled by Palmerston. The
jeu of the thing is rather amusing. Palmerston, who is thoroughly
versed in foreign affairs (while Lord John knows very little about
them), in every important case suggests to Lord John what to do.
Lord John brings it before the Cabinet as his own idea, and then
Palmerston supports him, as if the case was new to him.[3]

This is clearly overstated : for example, Russell was relatively
independent during the summer and autumn of 1860. But the
Prime Minister's hand is very obvious in the French alliance
proposals at the end of 1859 ; and he got his way, despite
Russell's original objections, over the sale of Venetia at the
end of 1860.

Hudson's influence, too, has been exaggerated. Russell did
not take Hudson's opinions at their face value. He knew very
well that they were simply Cavour's.[4] Late in 1859, indeed,
Palmerston and Russell tried to secure Hudson's nomination as
England's second representative at the proposed Congress.[5]

[1] RP PRO 30/22/66
[2] 22 March, Russell to Cowley (F.O. 27/1324), in *Further Correspondence
. . . Italy. Part IV* (State Papers. Session 24 January–28 August 1860.
Vol. lxvii. Command Paper No. 2656), pp. 6–10). 24 March, the same to
the same (CP F.O. 519/197)
[3] 19 October 1859 (*The Greville Memoirs*, vol. viii, pp. 269–70)
[4] e.g. 24 November 1859, Russell to Palmerston (BMS)
[5] *QVL* vol. iii, pp. 375–7

But it has already been shown that the Foreign Secretary had become very distrustful of Cavour by the time of the Sicilian expedition ; and he became equally distrustful of Hudson. Russell even wrote warning the Minister that he must take account of English as well as Piedmontese interests.[1] There is no evidence, however, that Russell intended to appoint Elliot Minister to the new Kingdom of Italy over Hudson's head, as *The Times* alleged at the instigation of Lord Shaftesbury.[2]

Not only have historians overestimated the influence of Russell and Hudson. They have also overrated the strength of the triumvirate in the Cabinet. For in fact the majority of Ministers was opposed to an active policy. And the majority had its way.

[1] 25 July (RP PRO 30/22/109)
[2] *History of 'The Times'*, vol. ii, pp. 337–8. See Hon. G. Elliot, *Sir James Hudson and Earl Russell* (London, 1886)

Conclusion

I

OF the three questions which this book attempts to answer, one has been disposed of. The Italian policy of England proves not to have been the decisive issue in the political crisis of 1859. The result of the General Election represented no special verdict of opinion ; and the Conservative Government was turned out by a straightforward party vote in the House of Commons. This change of Administration was peculiar, for this period, in that it was brought about, not by feeling against the Government on one particular issue, but by the reunion of the Liberal party.

II

In the formation of policy during the Italian crisis the Court played an exceptionally large part. The Queen stiffened Malmesbury's opposition to France ; she successfully fought for an inactive policy after Villafranca ; and during 1860 she even took the initiative in attempts to induce the Cabinet to unite against France. She curbed the private communications of Palmerston and Russell ; and she secured that they could not regularly act without Cabinet consent. In the case of the dispatch of 31 August 1860, however, she encouraged Russell to defy both Palmerston and the Cabinet.

Despite the great prestige and opportunities of their offices, the Prime Minister and Foreign Secretary in the Liberal

Cabinet often had to give way to their colleagues. The official policy in this case was a creation of the whole Cabinet. With the Conservatives, though Disraeli obviously had considerable influence, Derby and Malmesbury seem to have taken effective command.

Among English envoys abroad Cowley was easily the most important. He had a large share in policy-making under Malmesbury and also at the end of 1859 ; and his personal friendship with Napoleon III contributed greatly to ease Anglo-French relations. Hudson was too closely linked with Cavour for his views to be acceptable to the English Government ; but he was a valuable informant.

The influence of Parliament and public opinion is difficult to assess. It is clear that Derby and Malmesbury modified their policy in April–June 1859 to satisfy the obvious demand during the General Election for neutrality. Palmerston and Russell, in order to attain power, had to play down their sympathy with Italy and their readiness to act with France. It was necessary for them to join in the denunciation of the cession of Savoy and Nice in order to be able to ride the storm of popular indignation. And the dispatch of 27 October seems to represent a deliberate attempt to make amends for the dispatch of 31 August. Derby considered it essential to wait on the development of public opinion before taking the side of Austria ; Argyll made the same reservation in January 1860 about the French alliance. These are all cases where Ministers consciously adjusted their policies to take account of opinion.

However, the position of the Government was very strong. It is true that the public could in a sense exert steady pressure on the Cabinet, through the newspapers, pamphlets, books, petitions, meetings, and through Parliament. It is true also that in Parliament the technique of questions to Ministers was

by now well developed ; that as yet there were few restrictions
on the right of the private Member to make a nuisance of
himself ; that the 'sixties were the period of fullest publication
of Blue Books on foreign affairs ; and that some at least of
the Addresses to the Crown elicited documents—such as those
on the Savoy Question—which the Administration would
have preferred to withhold.[1] Moreover, there were regular,
though not frequent, full-dress debates. But even so the
Government was subject only to a very general surveillance.
The facts about events abroad could be known quickly. Not
so the facts about diplomacy and policy. In Parliament
Ministers seldom had to make comprehensive statements,
since they could plead the delicacy of the negotiations in
which they were engaged. The Parliamentary recess freed
the Government for several months from the need to explain
its policy, except for the occasional public speech. It was
not possible to print papers immediately they were requested ;
and they could, if necessary, be edited. That the Blue Books
contained very full sets of dispatches and telegrams was due
to the fact that the more embarrassing and compromising
communications were normally reserved for the private letters
of statesmen and envoys, which by custom remained secret.
Of those published during the Italian crisis, Malmesbury's
Blue Book was virtually complete [2] ; and the only important
omissions from the later collections were the dispatches about
the French alliance, presumably on the accepted ground that

[1] See A. J. P. Taylor, *The Trouble Makers* (London, 1957), p. 42 ;
P. Howarth, *Questions in the House* (London, 1956), esp. ch. vii ; Temperley
& Penson, *A Century of Diplomatic Blue Books*, Preface, esp. p. viii ; and
S. Lambert, ' The Influence of Parliament upon the Foreign Policy of the
Gladstone Government, 1868–74 ' (unpublished M.A. thesis, London University, 1949), summarised in *Bulletin of the Institute of Historical Research,*
vol. xxiii (1950), pp. 94–5, together with her article introducing select documents on ' The Presentation of Parliamentary Papers by the Foreign Office ',
ibid. pp. 76–83   [2] Hearder, *Rass. stor. del Ris.* (1956), pp. 49, 53–4

negotiations which had failed should not be disclosed.[1] Occasionally a dispatch was 'kept out of the office'. But the best protection of the Government was that emphasised by Granville in the House of Lords on 14 February 1860 : 'it was almost without precedent, if not irregular, to call for the production of Correspondence which the Government had stated it would not be for the public service at present to produce.'[2] Ministers could always secure delay. Private Members and the public could never learn much about the making of a policy ; and its precise nature was often not revealed, if at all, until too late for it to be modified. In most cases the time factor prevented Parliament and public opinion from exercising a very effective control. This is hardly surprising in view of the fact that even the Cabinet encountered the same difficulty.

It may be suggested, however, that it is often misleading to pit the Government against opinion. On Italian affairs there seems to have been a remarkable consensus of view among Englishmen. If so, it is understandable that the Cabinet was not always conscious of great pressure from outside. But Ministers were certainly accustomed to defer to what they identified as the voice of the people, or to what they guessed its future voice might be.

III

England's official policy during the Italian crisis was consistently ' pro-Italian '—in some sense. Her efforts to modify the Villafranca settlement, her advocacy of the annexation of the Duchies early in 1860 and her recognition of unification at the end of the year were obviously calculated to assist the

[1] Temperley & Penson, *A Century of Diplomatic Blue Books*, p. 567. See F.O. 27/1332 and 1333 etc. [2] *Parl. Deb.*, 3rd series, vol. clvi, col. 1011

Italian cause—even as understood by Cavour. But Malmesbury had believed he was acting in the true interests of Italy when he tried to satisfy her aspirations by obtaining from the existing states the promise of internal reforms, hoping thereby to frustrate what he regarded as a plot to impose French domination on the peninsula, the war against Austria. When Russell offered to support a compromise solution including an independent Central Italian Kingdom, he was under the impression that this was the best option available to the Italians at the time. When he recommended the alliance between Piedmont and Naples, and a dual political system for Italy, he supposed that he was helping to secure to Italy as much as would be controllable under a Liberal government and all that could be gained without further cessions to France. England did not always see the Italian Question in the same light as Italians did themselves. But she genuinely desired to procure for them the maximum possible degree of individual political freedom, and her policy always took into account their needs and their wishes. Ultimately she showed herself willing to accept the verdict of the inhabitants about their past and future rulers, even if her own advice was rejected.

Some actions of the English Government which were prompted by quite different considerations worked fortuitously in favour of the unification of the peninsula. Malmesbury's pressure on Prussia to remain neutral after the outbreak of the Franco-Austrian War was designed merely to localise that war, but in fact it had the effect of facilitating French victories. The advice to Naples to keep out of the war operated to discredit her still further in the eyes of Italian patriots : if she had then joined Piedmont, she would hardly have been annexed in 1860. It even seems reasonable to contend, as Gladstone late in life suggested, that the strengthening during the crisis of England's armed forces, due almost entirely to fear of France, gave added weight to Russell's approval of the *fait accompli* of unification.[1]

In the deliberations of the Cabinet before the official policy was agreed upon, it was by no means always the most pro-Italian members who recommended what proved to be the most pro-Italian policy. The Queen helped to prevent England's associating herself with a number of schemes which, if adopted, might have halted the process of unification : if, for example, Palmerston and Russell had had their way and had given moral support to the Emperor's pacification proposals before Villafranca, it would have been difficult for England to escape responsibility for guaranteeing the resulting settlement.[2] The Cabinet's opposition to the proposals for alliances with the German Powers was only to a limited extent motivated by Italian sympathies ; but it would obviously have been a severe blow to the prospects of unification if the treaties had been made.

Nor did the unofficial advice of Palmerston and Russell always point in the direction which later events showed to have been that leading to unification. In any case, the multiple policies which their opinions revealed must have helped to reduce the value of all England's counsels, official and unofficial, pro- and anti-Italian.

Unification came as a surprise. Palmerston thought it ' miraculous as no one in his senses or in his dreams cd have anticipated such continuous success '.[3] Russell's elation at the unexpected achievement was so great that he contradicted most of his previous dispatches in the remarkable manifesto of 27 October. Gladstone, after the event, described unification as ' among the greatest marvels of our time ' ; and he acknowledged that ' those were right who believed that, in

---

[1] Gladstone, *E.H.R.* (1887), p. 297   [2] Taylor, *E.H.R.* (1936), p. 73
[3] 10 November 1860, Clarendon to Cowley (CP F.O. 519/178)

the actual circumstances, the establishment of National unity was the true and only way to " local liberties ".'[1]

English policy, like that of all the Powers, was borne along by events. It is even arguable that the difference between the attitude of the Conservative and that of the Liberal Government was due largely to the changes in the situation in Italy. No-one was able to predict at all accurately the course of the Italian movement. England's policy-makers were often confused ; so was her attitude as shown to Europe. Her voice was as uncertain as any. She was, however, exceptionally quick to associate herself with the accomplished facts.

In reality England was not pursuing an Italian policy so much as a French policy. Malmesbury's discouragement of war was chiefly due to fear of the aggrandisement of France. On the other hand, England's influence in Italy, unless and until she decided to vie with France in furnishing material aid, depended on her ability to moderate the policy of Napoleon. For six months, from July 1859 to January 1860, the principal topic of Cabinet discussion in England was the possibility of some Anglo-French co-operation over Italy. When the annexation of Savoy and Nice put a close alliance out of the question, England's relations with France remained of prime importance : policy in 1860 was again dominated by fear of French aggrandisement, even though it was necessary to rely on the Emperor's goodwill in Italy.

Throughout 1859 and 1860 England avoided any new commitment in European affairs. The Conservative Government was prepared to join with France in guaranteeing Piedmont, but the offer was not accepted. Derby's Cabinet refused to intervene against Austria at the time of her ultimatum. Under Palmerston and Russell the Court and the Cabinet prevented any engagement with France or Piedmont ;

[1] Gladstone, *Gleanings of Past Years*, vol. iv, pp. 119n and 195n

and the Cabinet stopped alliances against France. When Spain was thought to be about to interfere, Palmerston was unable to obtain permission to proceed against her. France was threatened only with a protest if she tried to impede Garibaldi's progress ; and her assistance to the King of Naples at Gaeta provoked no English reprisals. Both Governments had been willing to go into Congresses, though without enthusiasm ; but neither would take stronger action. It is impossible to say whether England would have rescued the Italian cause if it had been in serious peril. But there is no reason to suppose that she was at any stage of the actual story ready to intervene on behalf of the Italians. The likelihood was perhaps greater that she would fight France, and so Italy. For both in April 1859 and in the spring of 1860 there was widespread fear of a ' drift ', like that of 1853–4, into such a war. Indeed it was often said that neutrality was preserved only because anti-French feeling was counterbalanced by Italian sympathy.

Probably, therefore, the best that Italians could ever have hoped for from England was ' moral support '. It was difficult for her at first to give rein to her sympathies with Italian Liberalism. For the military action which was a necessary preliminary to the attainment of Italian independence was bound to seem a threat to England's interests. Moreover, her ideological sympathy with Italian, and especially Piedmontese, constitutionalism and anti-Papalism entailed also antipathy to Piedmont's ally, despotic France, protectress of the Pope. Only after the war, in peaceful negotiations, could pro-Italian feeling and policy co-exist with English Francophobia.

Presumably, since unification came to pass, the Italians had received a sufficiency of moral support. Cavour and Garibaldi, and many of their compatriots, expressed great gratitude. The English were inclined to accept the thanks. As early as

CONCLUSION

26 October 1860 Palmerston spoke of the successful action ' of opinion, but opinion only ', in the affairs of Italy.[1] The case of Italian unification became the shining example of the possibilities of a non-interventionist foreign policy.

It has tended to be overlooked, however, that both Palmerston and Russell, and Gladstone too, had at the time regarded moral support by itself as inadequate. Their misgivings proved unjustified in this case. But the successful Italian precedent helped to ensure that the same pattern of policy and policy-making recurred in the Polish crisis of 1863 and the Schleswig-Holstein crisis of 1864, when circumstances were less favourable to England. On both occasions the Prime Minister and Foreign Secretary wished to take positive action, made public pronouncements in that sense, were overruled by the Cabinet, and had to recede. Gladstone ventured, after the Polish failure, to make the comparison between England's official policy towards Poland and that towards Italy :

Whether the case of Poland is parallel to the case of Italy . . . I will not undertake to say, but Her Majesty's Government have pursued the same policy in both instances. By an intervention strictly diplomatic, by the use of their good offices, by a plain expression of opinion, they have endeavoured to do what little good might lie in their power. . . . What we have had in view, with respect to Italy has been this,—that no Government ought to commit itself in any cause except where it is righteous, and that no cause is really righteous, with reference to its being taken up by Governments, unless the objects that are contemplated are practicable and attainable. . . . In regard to Italy, I don't think that my noble friends have at any time endeavoured to recommend anything beyond that which we believed to be strictly practicable and attainable. In the case of Poland, I am not aware that we have shrunk from recommending anything coming within the same description. . . . To repair a political wrong, or undo a

[1] *Leeds Mercury*, 27 October

political crime if it has long subsisted, is in many cases almost beyond the power of man. If in Italy we have hoped there might be redress for wrong inflicted through long generations, that has perhaps been a peculiarly happy case.[1]

It seems reasonable to retort that peculiarly happy cases make bad law.

The dominant aggressive mood of the 'fifties had by 1863 been superseded. The possibility of active intervention could not even be mentioned. Mr A. J. P. Taylor has put the point strikingly :

Cobden was the real Foreign Secretary of the early eighteen-sixties. He negotiated the Commercial treaty with France ; preached international arbitration ; and was the first to propose an agreed limitation of armaments. This is what he meant by *No foreign politics !* He could not believe in his own success. He wrote his longest and most carefully argued pamphlet, *The Three Panics*, against the anti-French alarms of 1860–1. The labour was unnecessary. The alarm was without reality, an echo of the past. . . .[2]

This is to exaggerate the swiftness of the change, and Cobden's part in it. Almost all Palmerston's old critics of the Don Pacifico debate and the Crimean War made their contribution : Tory isolationists, Francophobes, pacifists and, most numerous, the large body of moderate opinion, then best represented by the Peelites, who condemned Palmerston's ' spirit of interference '. The General Election of 1859, with its strong movement in favour of neutrality, was an important incident ; Malmesbury told Cowley that in a country ruled by the £10 householders *la grande politique* was impossible.[3] Assisted by this change of opinion, the Liberal Cabinet asserted control over the Prime Minister and the Foreign Secretary, and maintained it despite the very real alarm of

[1] *The Times*, 21 July 1863   [2] *The Trouble Makers*, pp. 64–5
[3] 3 June 1859 (CP F.O. 519/196)

1860. This was the chief significance of the Italian crisis in the history of English foreign policy : isolationism had triumphed.

At first the fact was not widely appreciated. It was obscured by the bombast of Palmerston and Russell, and by the apparent success of ' moral force ' in Italy. But already England spoke with a disembodied voice. The spirit of the two old statesmen was willing ; the Cabinet's flesh was weak. Sometimes, no doubt—in the case of Italy, perhaps—foreign Powers were impressed by the incantations of the spirit. But Bismarck had no time for the incorporeal.

Appendix

MINISTERS AND MINISTRIES
1830–1874

Prime Ministers		Foreign Secretaries	Party Complexion
Earl Grey	1830	Viscount Palmerston	Whig-Liberal
Viscount Melbourne	1834		
Sir Robert Peel	1834	Duke of Wellington	Conservative
Viscount Melbourne	1835	Viscount Palmerston	Whig-Liberal
Sir Robert Peel	1841	Earl of Aberdeen	Conservative
Lord John Russell	1846	Viscount Palmerston	Whig-Liberal
	1851	Earl Granville	
Earl of Derby	1852	Earl of Malmesbury	Conservative
Earl of Aberdeen	1852	Lord John Russell	Coalition :
	1853	Earl of Clarendon	Whig-Liberal and Peelite
Viscount Palmerston	1855	Earl of Clarendon	Whig-Liberal
Earl of Derby	1858	Earl of Malmesbury	Conservative
Viscount Palmerston	1859	Lord John (created Earl, 1861) Russell	Whig-Liberal
Earl Russell	1865	Earl of Clarendon	
Earl of Derby	1866	Lord Stanley	Conservative
Mr Disraeli	1868		
Mr Gladstone	1868–74	Earl of Clarendon 1868–70	Liberal
		Earl Granville 1870–4	

Bibliography

I   UNPUBLISHED SOURCES

MSS of QUEEN VICTORIA (Royal Archives, Windsor Castle)
          LORD PALMERSTON (Broadlands)
          LORD JOHN RUSSELL (Public Record Office)
          LORD COWLEY (Public Record Office)
          LORD GRANVILLE (Public Record Office)
          LORD CLARENDON (Bodleian Library)
          MR GLADSTONE (British Museum)
          SIR A. PANIZZI (British Museum)

FOREIGN OFFICE PAPERS (Public Record Office)
THE CORRESPONDENCE OF THE SARDINIAN LEGATION IN LONDON
     (Archivio del Ministero degli Affari Esteri, Rome)
THE GEORGE HOWELL COLLECTION (Bishopsgate Institute)
COLLECTION OF GLADSTONE'S SPEECHES AND PAMPHLETS
     (Hawarden Library, Chester)

II   CONTEMPORARY REFERENCE BOOKS AND OFFICIAL PUBLICATIONS

The Parliamentary Debates, 3rd series, vols. clii–clx
The Annual Register, 1859
The Dictionary of National Biography
Dod's Parliamentary Companion, 1858, 1859 and 1860

BLUE BOOKS

Session 31 May–13 August 1859 :

Accounts & Papers, vol. xxxii.   State Papers :
Correspondence relating to the Affairs of Italy, January to May 1859.
     Command Paper No. 2524.
Further Correspondence. . . . Command Paper No. 2527
Prussia (Neutrality) : Copy of a Despatch . . . 22 . . . June. . . .
     Return to an Address, No. 117
Further Despatch [7 July 1859]. . . . Command Paper No. 2550

BIBLIOGRAPHY

Session 24 January–28 August 1860 :

Accounts & Papers, vol. lxvii. State Papers :

Mémoire sur les Rapports entre La Suisse et La Savoie Neutralisée. Command Paper No. 2650

Dispatch from Earl Cowley . . . of 24 January. . . . Command Paper No. 2630

Correspondence respecting the proposed Annexation. . . . Command Paper No. 2624

Further Correspondence. . . . Part ii. Command Paper No. 2636
Further Correspondence. . . . Part iii. Command Paper No. 2638
Further Correspondence. . . . Part iv. Command Paper No. 2656
Further Correspondence. . . . Part v. Command Paper No. 2660
Further Correspondence. . . . Part vi. Command Paper No. 2702

Vol. lxviii. State Papers :

Correspondence relating to the Affairs of Italy, from . . . Villafranca to the Postponement of the Congress. Command Paper No. 2609

Correspondence respecting . . . Naples. Command Paper No. 2642

Dispatches relating to the . . . Expedition . . . to the Kingdom of the Two Sicilies. Command Paper No. 2672

Correspondence respecting the landing of General Garibaldi. . . . Command Paper No. 2674

Further Correspondence. . . . Command Paper No. 2683

Correspondence. . . . Sicily. Command Paper No. 2687

Session 5 February–6 August 1861 :

Accounts & Papers, vol. lxvii. State Papers :

Further Correspondence . . . Italy. Part vii. Command Paper No. 2757

Further Correspondence . . . Italy. Part viii. Command Paper No. 2787

Further Correspondence . . . Italy. Part ix. Command Paper No. 2804

BIBLIOGRAPHY

III CONTEMPORARY PERIODICALS, PAMPHLETS AND ARTICLES

The Times
The Daily News
The Leeds Express
The Leeds Intelligencer
The Leeds Mercury
The Newcastle Chronicle
The Newcastle Courant
The Newcastle Guardian
The Newcastle Journal
The Birmingham Daily Post

The Birmingham Saturday Evening Post
The Birmingham Journal
The Worcestershire Chronicle
The Economist
The Quarterly Review
The Edinburgh Review
The Saturday Review
The Westminster Review
Fraser's Magazine
Punch

ACTON, LORD. ' Cavour ', in *Historical Essays and Studies*, London 1908 (1861)
— ' Nationality ', in *The History of Freedom and Other Essays*, London 1902 (1862)
ARNOLD, M. *England and the Italian Question*, London 1859
COBDEN, R. *The Three Panics*, London 1862
GLADSTONE, W. E. ' The Declining Efficiency of Parliament ', *Quarterly Review*, vol. c, 1856
— ' Farini's *Stato Romano* ', *Edinburgh Review*, vol. xcv, 1852
— ' France and the Late Ministry ', *Quarterly Review*, vol. ciii, 1858
— *Gleanings of Past Years*, 4 vols., London 1879
— ' The History of 1852–60, and Greville's Latest Journals ', *English Historical Review*, vol. ii, 1887
— *Two Letters to the Earl of Aberdeen, on the State Prosecutions of the Neapolitan Government*, London 1851
— ' The New Parliament and its Work ', *Quarterly Review*, vol. ci, 1857
— ' The Past and Present Administrations ', *Quarterly Review*, vol. civ, 1858
— ' Prospects Political and Financial ', *Quarterly Review*, vol. ci, 1857
— ' Sardinia and Rome ', *Quarterly Review*, vol. xcviii, 1855
— ' War in Italy ', *Quarterly Review*, vol. cv, 1859
— ' The Works and Life of Giacomo Leopardi ', *Quarterly Review*, vol. lxxxvi, 1850
MILL, J. S. ' A Few Words on Non-Intervention ', *Fraser's Magazine*, vol. lx, 1859

IV PUBLISHED CORRESPONDENCE AND DIARIES

BASSETT, A. T. (ed.) *Gladstone to his Wife*, London 1936

BENSON, A. C., & ESHER, VISCOUNT (ed.) *The Letters of Queen Victoria, 1837–61*, 3 vols., London 1908

BIANCHI, N. *La politique du Comte Camille de Cavour de 1852 à 1861*, Turin 1885

CADDEO, R. (ed.) *Epistolario di Carlo Cattaneo*, Florence 1949–56

Cavour e l'Inghilterra, 2 vols., Bologna 1933

Il Carteggio Cavour-Nigra dal 1858 al 1861, 4 vols., Bologna 1926–9

CHIALA, L. (ed.) *Lettere edite ed inedite di Camillo Cavour*, 6 vols., Turin 1883–7

— *Politica segreta di Napoleone III e di Cavour in Italia e in Ungheria*, Turin 1895

CIAMPINI, R. (ed.) *Il '59 in Toscana*, Florence 1958

COLOMBO, A. (ed.) *Carteggi e Documenti Diplomatici inediti di Emanuele d'Azeglio*, 2 vols. (vol. ii ' non ultimato, edizione fuori commercio ' ; vol. i, Turin 1920)

COOK, E. T., & WEDDERBURN, A. (ed.) *The Works of John Ruskin*, 39 vols., London 1903–12

CURATO, F. (ed.) *Le Relazioni Diplomatiche tra la Gran Bretagna ed il Regno di Sardegna, 1852–6*, 2 vols., Turin 1956

D'IDEVILLE, H. *Journal d'un Diplomate en Italie : Turin 1859–62*, Paris 1872

GOOCH, G. P. (ed.) *The Later Correspondence of Lord John Russell*, 2 vols., London 1925

GREVILLE, C. C. F. *A Journal of the Reign of Queen Victoria from 1852 to 1860*, 2 vols., London 1887 [*The Greville Memoirs*, vols vii & viii]

GUEDALLA, P. (ed.) *Gladstone and Palmerston*, London 1928

HÜBNER, COMTE DE. *Neuf Ans de Souvenirs d'un Ambassadeur d'Autriche à Paris sous le Second Empire, 1851–9*, 2 vols., Paris 1904

JAGOW, K. (ed.) *Letters of the Prince Consort*, London 1938

JOHNSON, A. H. (ed.) *Letters of Charles Greville and Henry Reeve, 1836–65*, London 1924

KENNEDY, A. L. (ed.) ' *My Dear Duchess*', *Social and Political Letters to the Duchess of Manchester, 1858–1869*, London 1956

KENYON, F. G. (ed.) *Letters of Elizabeth Barrett Browning*, 2 vols., London 1897

LEWIS, SIR G. F. (ed.) *Letters of Sir George Cornewall Lewis*, London 1870

MALLOCK, W. H., & RAMSDEN, LADY GWENDOLEN (ed.) *Letters, etc. of Twelfth Duke of Somerset*, London 1893

BIBLIOGRAPHY

MASSARI, G. *Diario dalle cento voci 1858–60*, Bologna 1959
Scritti editi ed inediti di G. Mazzini, Imola 1906–
NOBILI, M., & CAMERANI, S. (ed.) *Carteggi di Bettino Ricasoli*, Rome 1939–
RICHARDS, E. F. (ed.) *Mazzini's Letters to an English Family*, 3 vols., London 1920–2
Letters of Lord St. Maur and Lord Edward St. Maur, 1846 to 1859, London 1888
WALLING, R. A. J. (ed.) *The Diaries of John Bright*, London 1930

V BIOGRAPHIES, AUTOBIOGRAPHIES AND MEMOIRS*

The Education of Henry Adams, New York 1931
AIRLIE, COUNTESS OF. *Lady Palmerston*, 2 vols., London 1922
(ALATRI, P.) [see under Romano]
ARESE, F. *Cavour e le Strade Ferrate*, Milan 1953
ARGYLL, 8TH DUKE OF. *Autobiography and Memoirs*, 2 vols., London 1906
ASHLEY, HON. E. *The Life of Henry John Temple, Viscount Palmerston*, 2 vols., London 1876
AUCHMUTY, J. J. 'Acton's Election as an Irish Member of Parliament', *English Historical Review*, vol. lxi, 1946
BARRINGTON, E. I. *The Servant of All*, 2 vols., London 1927
BASSETT, A. T. *Gladstone's Speeches*, London 1916
BEALES, D. E. D. 'Gladstone on the Italian Question, January 1860', *Rassegna storica del Risorgimento*, vol. xli, 1954
BELL, H. C. F. *Lord Palmerston*, 2 vols., London 1936
BROOKS, C. *Antonio Panizzi*, Manchester 1931
BUCKLE, G. E. See MONYPENNY, W. F.
CHAMBERS, O. W. S. *Garibaldi and Italian Unity*, London 1864
COOK, SIR E. T. *Delane of 'The Times'*, London 1915
DASENT, A. I. *The Life of J. T. Delane*, 2 vols., London 1908
DAVIES, W. W. *Gladstone and the Unification of Italy*, London 1918
DAWSON, W. H. *Richard Cobden and Foreign Policy*, London 1926
EVANS, H. *Sir Randal Cremer, His Life and Work*, London 1909
FAGAN, L. *The Life of Sir Anthony Panizzi*, 2 vols., London 1880
FINIGAN, L. *The Life of Peter Stuart, the 'Ditton Doctor'*, London 1921
FITZMAURICE, LORD EDMOND. *The Life of 2nd Earl Granville*, 2 vols., London 1905

* This section includes books and articles dealing with a particular aspect or period of the career of an individual. Many of the biographies contain otherwise unpublished material from private archives.

180

GALANTE, A. *La Politica Estera di G. Gladstone*, Bologna 1917

GASH, N. 'Peel and the Party System, 1830–50', *Transactions of the Royal Historical Society*, 5th series, vol. i, 1951

GOPAL, S. 'Gladstone and the Italian Question', *English Historical Review*, vol. xli, 1956

GRIFFITH, G. O. *Mazzini: Prophet of Modern Europe*, London 1932

GUEDALLA, P. *Palmerston*, London 1926

GUERZONI, G. *Garibaldi*, 2 vols., Florence 1882

HALES, E. E. Y. *Mazzini and the Secret Societies*, London 1956
— *Pio Nono*, London 1954

HAMMOND, J. L., & B. *James Stansfeld*, London 1932

HANCOCK, W. K. *Ricasoli and the Risorgimento in Tuscany*, London 1926

HEARDER, H. 'The Foreign Policy of Lord Malmesbury, 1858–9', unpublished Ph.D. Dissertation, 1954 (Institute of Historical Research)
— 'La Politica di Lord Malmesbury verso l'Italia nella Primavera del 1859', *Rassegna storica del Risorgimento*, vol. xliii, 1956

HERZEN, A. I. *My Past and Thoughts*, 6 vols., London 1924

HODDER, E. *The Life and Work of the Seventh Earl of Shaftesbury*, 3 vols., London 1886

HOLYOAKE, G. J. *Sixty Years of an Agitator's Life*, 2 vols., London 1892

HUDSON, D. *Martin Tupper*, London 1949

HUMPHREY, A. W. *Robert Applegarth*, London 1914

IMLAH, A. H. *Lord Ellenborough*, Cambridge (Mass.), 1939

JONES, E. R. *The Life and Speeches of Joseph Cowen*, London 1885

JONES, W. D. *Lord Derby and Victorian Conservatism*, Oxford 1956

KING, BOLTON. *The Life of Mazzini*, London 1912

KNAPLUND, P. A. *Gladstone's Foreign Policy*, New York 1935

KOSSUTH, L. *Memories of My Exile*, London 1880

LACAITA, C. *An Italian Englishman*, London 1933

LAUGHTON, J. K. *Memoirs of the Life and Correspondence of Henry Reeve*, 2 vols., London 1898

LE MAY, G. F. H. 'Mr Gladstone and Italy, to 1874', Gladstone Prize Essay, 1951 (Oxford University)

LOFTUS, LORD AUGUSTUS. *Diplomatic Reminiscences*, 2 vols., London 1892

LUCAS, R. *Lord Glenesk and the 'Morning Post'*, London 1910

MACCARTHY, D., & RUSSELL, LADY AGATHA (ed.) *Lady John Russell, A Memoir*, London 1926

MACK SMITH, D. *Garibaldi*, London 1957

MAGNUS, P. *Gladstone*, London 1954

MALMESBURY, 3RD EARL OF. *Memoirs of an Ex-Minister*, London 1885

MARTIN, B. K. *The Triumph of Lord Palmerston*, London 1924

MARTIN, SIR T. *The Life of H.R.H. the Prince Consort*, 5 vols., London 1875–80

MARTINEAU, J. *The Life of Henry Pelham, Fifth Duke of Newcastle*, London 1908

MATTER, P. *Cavour et l'Unité italienne*, 3 vols., Paris 1927

MAXWELL, SIR H. E. *The Life and Letters of the Fourth Earl of Clarendon*, 2 vols., London 1913

MONYPENNY, W. F., & BUCKLE, G. E. *The Life of Benjamin Disraeli*, 6 vols., London 1910–24

MORELLI, E. *Mazzini in Inghilterra*, Florence 1938

MORLEY, J. *The Life of Richard Cobden*, London 1903

— *The Life of William Ewart Gladstone*, 3 vols., London 1903

PARKER, C. S. *The Life and Letters of Sir James Graham*, 2 vols., London 1907

PEMBERTON, W. B. *Lord Palmerston*, London 1954

ROMANO, PAOLO (P. ALATRI). *Silvio Spaventa*, Bari 1942

RUMBOLD, SIR H. *Recollections of a Diplomatist*, 2 vols., London 1902

SACERDOTE, G. *La Vita di Giuseppe Garibaldi*, Milan 1933

SMITH, B. A. *Dean Church*, Oxford 1958

STANMORE, LORD. *A Memoir of Sidney Herbert*, 2 vols., London 1906

THAYER, W. R. *The Life and Times of Cavour*, 2 vols., Boston 1911

THOMPSON, J. M. *Louis Napoleon and the Second Empire*, Oxford 1954

TREVELYAN, G. M. *The Life of John Bright*, London 1913

— *Garibaldi and the Thousand*, London 1909

— *Garibaldi and the Making of Italy*, London 1912

TROLLOPE, A. *Lord Palmerston*, London 1882

VIDLER, A. R. *The Orb and the Cross*, London 1945

WALPOLE, S. *The Life of Lord John Russell*, 2 vols., London 1889

WEBSTER, SIR C. K. *The Foreign Policy of Palmerston, 1830–41*, 2 vols., London 1951

WELLESLEY, HON. F. A. *The Paris Embassy during the Second Empire*, London 1928

WHYTE, A. J. *The Political Life and Letters of Cavour, 1848–1861*, Oxford 1930

WILLIAMS, W. E. *The Rise of Gladstone to the Leadership of the Liberal Party, 1859–68*, Cambridge 1934

YOUNG, G. M. *Mr Gladstone*, Oxford 1944

ZUMBINI, B. *W. E. Gladstone nelle sue Relazioni con l'Italia*, Bari 1914

VI OTHER SECONDARY WORKS

A. *The European Background*

BINKLEY, R. C. *Realism and Nationalism, 1852–71*, London 1935
BLUMBERG, A. 'Russian Policy and the Franco-Austrian War of 1859', *Journal of Modern History*, vol. xxvi, 1954
CASE, L. M. *Franco-Italian Relations, 1860–65*, Philadelphia 1932
— *French Opinion on War and Diplomacy during the Second Empire*, Philadelphia 1954
D'ENTRÈVES, E. P. *L'Ultima Battaglia Politica di Cavour*, Turin 1956
ENGEL VON JANOSI, F. *L'Ultimatum Austriaco del 1859*, Rome 1938
HALLBERG, C. W. *Franz Joseph and Napoleon III*, New York 1955
MACK SMITH, D. *Cavour and Garibaldi 1860*, Cambridge 1954
— 'Cavour's attitude to Garibaldi's expedition to Sicily', *Cambridge Historical Journal*, vol. ix, 1949
— 'Vittorio Emanuele e i suoi Primi Ministri', *Rassegna storica del Risorgimento*, vol. ix, 1954
MONNIER, L. *L'Annexion de la Savoie à la France et la Politique Suisse, 1860*, Geneva 1932
MOSSE, W. E. *The European Powers and the German Question, 1848–71*, Cambridge 1958
— 'The Russians at Villafranca', *Slavonic Review*, vol. xxx, 1952
MAZZIOTTI, M. *Napoleone III e l'Italia*, Milan 1925
OMODEO, A. *Difesa del Risorgimento*, Turin 1955
PISCHEDDA, C. 'L'attività politica del Cavour dopo Villafranca', in *Scritti Vari*, vol. ii, Turin 1950
POUTHAS, C. H. 'La médiation de Napoléon III entre le Roi de Naples, les Siciliens et le Gouvernement Piémontais (Mai–Août 1860)', *Rassegna storica del Risorgimento*, vol. xxxix, 1952
SILVA, P. *Italia, Francia, Inghilterra nel Mediterraneo*, Milan 1936
— *Il Mediterraneo dall'Unità di Roma all'Unità d'Italia*, Milan 1933
SUMNER, B. H. 'The Secret Franco-Russian Treaty of 3 March 1859', *English Historical Review*, vol. xlviii, 1933
TAYLOR, A. J. P. 'European Mediation and the Agreement of Villafranca, 1859', *English Historical Review*, vol. li, 1936
— *The Italian Problem in European Diplomacy, 1847–1849*, Manchester 1934
— *The Struggle for Mastery in Europe, 1848–1918*, Oxford 1954

VALSECCHI, F. *La Mediazione Europea e la Definizione dell'Aggressore alla Vigilia della Guerra del 1859*, Rome 1938

ZAZO, A. *La Politica Estera del Regno delle Due Sicilie nel 1859–60*, Naples 1940

B. *The English Background*

APPLEMAN, P., MADDEN, W. A., & WOLFF, M. '*1859*': *Entering an Age of Crisis*, Bloomington, 1959

BAGEHOT, W. *The English Constitution*, Oxford 1928

BEVINGTON, M. M. *The 'Saturday Review'*, New York 1941

BRIGGS, A. *The Age of Improvement*, London 1959

— *Victorian People*, London 1954

BROCK, P. 'Polish Democrats and English Radicals, 1832–62', *Journal of Modern History*, vol. xxv, 1953

CARR, E. H. *The Romantic Exiles*, London 1933

CLAPHAM, J. H. *An Economic History of Modern Britain*, 3 vols., Cambridge 1926–38, (vol. ii)

GASH, N. *Politics in the Age of Peel*, London 1952

GILLESPIE, F. E. *Labor and Politics in England, 1850–67*, Durham (N. Carolina, U.S.A.) 1927

GLEASON, J. H. *The Genesis of Russophobia in Great Britain*, Cambridge (Mass.) 1950

HALÉVY, E. *The Age of Peel and Cobden*, London 1947

HANHAM, H. J. *Elections and Party Management: Politics in the Time of Disraeli and Gladstone*, London 1959

— 'The General Election of 1868', unpublished Ph.D. Dissertation, 1953 (Cambridge University Library)

HENDERSON, G. B. *Crimean War Diplomacy*, Glasgow 1947

HIRST, F. W. *The Six Panics and Other Essays*, London 1913

The History of 'The Times', 5 vols., London 1935–52 (vol. ii)

HOWARTH, P. *Questions in the House*, London 1956

JENNINGS, SIR W. I. *Cabinet Government*, Cambridge 1959

JOLL, J. (ed.) *Britain and Europe, 1793–1940*, London 1950

LAMBERT, S. 'The Influence of Parliament upon the Foreign Policy of the Gladstone Government, 1868–74', unpublished M.A. Dissertation, 1949 (Institute of Historical Research)

— 'The Presentation of Parliamentary Papers by the Foreign Office', *Bulletin of the Institute of Historical Research*, vol. xxiii, 1950

BIBLIOGRAPHY

Low, S., & Sanders, L. C. *The Political History of England*, vol. xii, London 1907

Lowell, A. L. *The Government of England*, 2 vols., London 1912

Maccoby, S. *English Radicalism, 1832–52*, London 1935
— *English Radicalism, 1853–86*, London 1938

Mackay, D. F. 'The Influence of the Italian Risorgimento on British "Public Opinion" . . . 1859–61', unpublished D.Phil. Dissertation, 1959 (Bodleian Library)

Paul, Sir H. *A History of Modern England*, 5 vols., London 1904, (vol. ii)

Sebag-Montefiore, C. *A History of the Volunteer Forces*, London 1908

Seton-Watson, R. W. *Britain in Europe, 1789–1914*, Cambridge 1938

Stuart, C. H. 'The Formation of the Coalition Cabinet of 1852', *Transactions of the Royal Historical Society*, 5th Series, vol. iv, 1954

A. J. P. Taylor. *The Trouble Makers*, London 1957

Temperley, H. W. V. *England and the Near East, The Crimea*, London 1936
— & Penson, L. M. *A Century of Diplomatic Blue Books*, Cambridge 1938
— — (ed.) *Foundations of British Foreign Policy*, Cambridge 1938

Whyte, J. H. *The Independent Irish Party*, Oxford 1958

Woodward, E. L. *The Age of Reform, 1815–1870*, Oxford 1938

Young, G. M. (ed.) *Early Victorian England*, 2 vols., Oxford 1934

C. *Other Works*

Anderson, M. A. 'The Character of British Relations with France, 1859–65', unpublished M.A. Dissertation, 1949 (Institute of Historical Research)

Avetta, M. 'Studi Cavouriani I : Una "vexata quaestio" alla luce dei carteggi cavouriani', *Rassegna storica del Risorgimento*, vol. xxi (i), 1934

Baxter, J. P. *The Introduction of the Ironclad Warship*, Cambridge (Mass.) 1933

Bevington, M. M. (ed.) *Matthew Arnold's 'England and the Italian Question'*, Durham, (N. Carolina, U.S.A.) 1953

Blakiston, N. 'L'Inghilterra e la tariffa piemontese', *Rassegna storica del Risorgimento*, vol. xliv, 1957

Brand, C. P. *Italy and the English Romantics*, Cambridge 1957

The Cambridge History of British Foreign Policy, 1783–1919. Ed. Sir A. W. Ward & G. P. Gooch, 3 vols., Cambridge 1923 (vol. ii)

The Cambridge Modern History. Ed. Sir A. W. Ward, Sir G. W. Prothero & Sir S. Leathers, 13 vols., Cambridge 1934 (vol. xi)

Colombo, A. *L'Inghilterra nel Risorgimento italiano*, Milan 1917

COVILLE, A., & TEMPERLEY, H. W. V. (ed.) *Studies in Anglo-French History*, Cambridge 1935

DE GROOT, E. 'The Florentine Tragedy of Mr Mather of South Shields ', *Durham University Journal*, vol. xliv, 1952

DUNHAM, A. L. *The Anglo-French Treaty of Commerce of 1860 and the Progress of the Industrial Revolution in France*, Michigan 1930

ELLIOT, HON. G. *Sir James Hudson and Earl Russell*, London 1886

GUTTSMAN, W. L. 'The General Election of 1859 in the Cities of Yorkshire', *International Review of Social History*, vol. ii, 1957

HALE, J. R. *England and the Italian Renaissance*, London 1954

Italia e Inghilterra nel Risorgimento, Italian Institute of London Publications, No. 3, London 1954

LEY, H. *Die italienische Einigung und die englische Politik, 1859–61*, Leipzig 1935

MORELLI, E. (ed.) *Italia e Inghilterra nella prima fase del Risorgimento*, Rome 1952

PAGÉS, G. 'The Annexation of Savoy and the Crisis in Anglo-French Relations, January to April 1860', in Coville & Temperley, *Studies in Anglo-French History*

ROSSELLI, N. *Inghilterra e regno di Sardegna dal 1815 al 1847*, Turin 1954

RUDMAN, H. W. *Italian Nationalism and English Letters*, London 1940

SIGNORETTI, A. *Italia e Inghilterra durante il Risorgimento*, Milan 1940

SPINI, G. *Risorgimento e Protestanti*, Naples 1956

TREVELYAN, G. M. *Englishmen and Italians*, London 1919

TREVES, G. A. *The Golden Ring*, London 1956

URBAN, M. B. *British Opinion and Policy on the Unification of Italy, 1856–1861*, Scottdale (Pa., U.S.A.) 1938

Index

Aberdeen, city of, 128
— 4th Earl of, 56, 90, 91 ; Gladstone's *Letters* to, 27, 32. *See also* Government
Achilli, G., 23
Administration. *See* Government
Administrative Reform, 13, 14
Adriatic Sea, 62 ; English policy and, 57, 64, 119, 155
Albert, Prince Consort, 39, 116, 125, 156 ; views on domestic politics, 28, 66, 70, 76 ; views on Italian Question, 28, 63, 66, 145 ; on Granville's attempt to form a Government, 85 ; relations with Clarendon, 85, 99 ; on Palmerston's Government (1859), 92 ; influence on foreign policy of Palmerston's Government, general, 98–9, 106 ; communications with Granville, 97, 99, 100, 103, 106, 116*n*, 125, 135, 141 ; communications with Sir George Grey, 99 ; communications with Lewis and Newcastle, 99, 114 ; communications with Wood, 99, 114*n*, 116, 139–40, 158 ; and Gladstone, 126. *See also* Victoria
Alliances, English, 31
— — with Austria, feared, 56
— — with France, 3, 20, 38, 44, 45, 51–2, 70, 80, 108, 156, 164, 165, 169 ; proposals to revive, 45, 107, 112, 116, 136, 142, 161 ; rejected by England, 45, 124–5, 136 ; English Government considers renewing (September 1859–January 1860), 110, 112–27 ; general arguments in favour of, 110–11, 119, 120–1 ; and England's Italian policy, general, 111–12 ; prospect fades, 131, 132, 139, 143–145, 158–9, 169

Alliances, English, with German Powers, projected, 139–43, 160, 168
— — with Piedmont, 1855, 3, 34 ; proposals to revive, with France, 45, 71, 116, 119–21 ; proposals to revive, against France, 149, 150, 152
— — with Russia, proposed, 63
— French, with Austria, feared, 123 ; with Piedmont, 3, 4–6, 36–7, 170 ; with Russia, suspected, 39, 41, 51, 64, 65–6, 123, 141
— Holy, 119, 155
— Neapolitan, with Piedmont, 150, 152, 167
America : South, 26 ; United States of, 84 ; Civil War in, 11, 14
Annexation. *See* Central Italy, Lombardy, Naples, Savoy and Nice, Sicily
Anti-Corn-Law League, 12, 13
Argyll, 8th Duke of, 86 ; attitude to Italian Question, 92, 105, 106, 117, 121–2 ; on public opinion and the French alliance, 129, 164
Arnold, M., 68
Austria : and Italian affairs, xv, ch. I, 34, 36–46 *passim*, 49, 56, 101, 113, 117, 141 ; English attitudes to, 9–10, 21, 24, 25, 28, 29, 34, ch. III *passim*, 61, 62–5, 68, 70–2, 75, 80–1, 91–6, 100–27 *passim*, 135, 140–3, 148, 156, 157, 167, 168, 169 ; ultimatum to Piedmont (April 1859), 41, 45, 62–5, 70, 94. *See also* Alliances, England, Lombardy, Venetia
Avetta, M., historian, vii, 154*n*
Azeglio, E. d', Piedmontese Minister in London, 57, 109, 135, 150, 153 ; on English attitudes to the Italian Question, 24, 50, 71, 143, 151, 155–6

187

INDEX

141, 142, 146–54, 158, 159, 160, 167

England, foreign policy of, and Papal State, 40–1, 100, 125
— — — and Piedmont, 35, 39, 41–5, 55, 64, 102–9, 113, 115–16, 119–22, 126–7, 134–9, 148–59, 169
— — — and Polish Question, 171
— — — and Prussia, 39, 40, 49, 63–4, 67, 99–100, 118, 139–43, 155–6, 167, 168
— — — and Russia, 39, 40, 63, 64, 70, 71, 118, 140–1, 156
— — — and Spain, 156–7 and 157n
— — — Conservative and Liberal compared, 35, 57–8, 59, 67, 69–72, 81, 99, 113, 169–70
— — — constitutional role of Foreign Secretary and Prime Minister in formation of, 97–8
— — — general considerations behind, xv, 35, 37–9, 110–12, 147
— — — importance as an issue, in general election (1859), 69–72, 74–5, 163 ; in Liberals' negotiations, 78–80 ; in no-confidence debate, 81–4, 163
See also Alliances, Cabinet, Commercial treaty, Government, Parliament

Exiles : English, in Italy, 22 ; Italian, in England, 32–3, 56 ; Italian, in Piedmont, 3

Faucigny, 136, 138
Federation, schemes for Italian, 5–6, 36, 101, 102, 126, 136
Ferdinand II. See Naples
Flahaut, Count, 138
Florence, 22, 24, 103
Foreign policy, English. See England, Government
France, 19, 91 ; and Italian affairs, 4–8, 34–5, 36–45 passim, 49, 62, 100–1, 104, 107, 109, 112–17, 124, 126, 131–7 passim, 143, 150, 152, 153, 154, 170 ; and Papal State, 37, 40, 41, 116–17, 125, 170 ; divided policy of, 37 ; English attitudes to, 9, 10, 11, 17, 20, 28, 29, 32, 37–45, 48–61 passim, 62–8, 70–1, 80–1, 92, 94–6, 100–59 passim, 166, 167,

169–70. See also Alliances, Commercial treaty, England
Francis II. See Naples
Free Trade, 12, 14, 16, 20, 25–6, 48, 86. See Commercial treaty

Gaeta, 154, 170
Garibaldi, G. : character, 27 ; expedition to Sicily and Naples, 7, 8, 145–6 ; relations with Cavour, 8, 148, 149 ; admired in England, 9, 24–5, 26–7, 28 ; English attitudes to his expedition, 146–55, 158, 160, 170 ; visit to London, 1864, 13, 33
Gavazzi, A., 23
General elections, 15, 72–3, 82–3
— — (1857), 11, 13, 15, 17, 18, 72, 73
— — (1859), xv, 68–75, 127 ; effect on foreign policy, 70–1, 164
— — in Ireland, 74–5 ; movement for neutrality during, 67–8, 70–1, 80–1, 172 ; result of, 73–4, 77 ; significance of result of, 73–4, 75, 77, 92, 163, 172
See also Parliament
Genoa, 32, 145, 149, 151
Germany, 21, 63, 135. See also Austria, Prussia
Gibraltar, 120, 144
Gibson, T. M., M.P., 86, 92, 117
Gladstone, W. E., M.P., 20, 32, 33, 92, 167 ; papers, vii ; financial policy, 13, 87, 90, 132–3, 134, 138 ; views on Italian Question, 21, 29, 33, 34, 53, 58, 91, 96–7, 99, 105, 117–19, 123, 126–7, 132, 139, 141, 142, 147, 155–6, 159, 168–9, 171–2 ; on Papacy, 23, 96, 119, 126 ; on public opinion, 25, 34, 53–5, 129–30, 132, 133, 139 ; and Naples, 27, 91 ; Letters to Lord Aberdeen, 27, 32 ; visits Cavour (1859), 53, 55 ; political position in 1859, 76, 82, 84 and n, 86–91 ; accepts office, 86 ; relations with Disraeli, 90 ; role in Palmerston's Cabinet, 96, 99, 105, 122, 132–3, 144 ; and French alliance, 110, 117–20, 123, 144 ; and commercial treaty, 117, 131–3,

139, 144 ; threatens to resign, 124.
See also Palmerston
Gooch, G.P., historian, 74*n*, 149*n*, 156*n*
Government, of 1841–6 (Sir Robert
Peel's), 16, 18
— of 1846–52 (Lord John Russell's),
34 ; 1851 crisis, 16 ; fall, 10, 14, 15
— of 1852–5 (Lord Aberdeen's), 16 ;
fall, 10–11, 14, 15, 17, 84
— of 1855–8 (Lord Palmerston's),
16, 34–5 ; 1857 crisis, 11, 13, 15,
84 ; fall, 11, 13, 15
— of 1858–9 (Lord Derby's), xv,
76, 85, 90 ; defeat on Parliamentary Reform (31 March 1859),
58–9, 69, 72, 82 ; fall, 14, 82–4 ;
foreign policy, 35, 39–45, 46, 48–9,
57, 61–4, 70–1, 99, 146, 166, 167,
169–70 ; policy formation, 45–9,
58–61, 70–1, 163, 164 ; public
opinion and, 48–9, 57, 59–61,
70–1, 80–1, 164 ; sounds Opposition, 47, 59
— of 1859–65 (Lord Palmerston's),
xv, 46, 84, 92, 93 ; formation of,
16, 79, 85–6, 92, 127 ; break-up
threatened (1860), 120, 122–5,
128 ; difficulties (1864), 11 ; foreign
policy, 99–127, 131–60, 166–73 ;
policy formation, general, 96–9,
160–2, 163–4 ; public opinion and,
127–30, 132–5, 138–9, 159–60, 164
— change of (1859), xv, 53, 75, 85,
92, 163
See also Alliances, Cabinet, England, House of Commons, Parliament.
Governments : and dissolution, 15,
73 ; and public opinion, general,
5, 14–15, 17–19, 59, 164–6 ;
Derby's of 1858–9 and Palmerston's
of 1859–65, compared, 35, 46, 93,
128, 164, 169–70 ; minority, 15,
58–9, 72 ; table of Ministers and
(1830–74), 175 ; weakness of, in
Age of Palmerston, 14–16, 18–19.
See also Alliances, Cabinet, England, House of Commons, Parliament
Graham, Sir James, M.P., 76, 78, 86,
90, 132
Granville, 2nd Earl, 78, 86, 92, 166 ;

attempts to form a Government,
85 ; role in Palmerston's Cabinet,
97, 99 ; communications with
Prince Albert on divisions in Palmerston's Cabinet, 97, 99 and *n*,
100, 103, 106, 116*n*, 125, 135,
141 ; other letters on same subject,
107, 117, 118, 123
Greece, 10, 14
Greville, Hon. C. C. F., 55, 58, 68,
73, 129–30, 161
Grey, 2nd Earl, 13, 16
Grey, General C., 99 and *n*
Grey, Sir George, 86, 92, 99 and *n*,
102, 123, 141

Hanover, 14
Haynau, General, 9
Hayter, W. G., M.P., 73
Hearder, H., historian, vii, 36*n*
Herbert, Hon. S., M.P., 76, 82*n*, 86 ; on
parties (1859), 18–19 ; on political
situation (1859), 77 ; efforts to
reunite Liberal party, 78–80 ; account of Liberal party meeting,
79–80 ; attitude to Italian Question, 92, 105, 123, 127 ; on public
opinion, 129
Home Office, 30, 86
Horsman, E., M.P., 79–80, 82, 84
House of Commons, 10, 11, 71, 124,
140, 161 ; power of, 15–16, 75 ;
and public opinion, 17–18, 52–3,
107 ; state in 1859, 41, 57–8,
76–7 ; and foreign policy, 59,
127–8, 159–60 ; full complement
of M.P.s, 72 ; influence on Palmerston, 107. *See also* Parliament
House of Lords, 10, 41, 59, 127,
166. *See also* Parliament
Hübner, Count, Austrian Ambassador in Paris, 36 and *n*, 63
Hudson, Sir James, English Minister
in Turin, 39, 53, 109, 134, 152 ;
attitude to Italian Question, 33,
103, 108, 142, 145, 147, 151 ;
Malmesbury and, 44, 47 ; Russell
and, 103, 160–2 ; and proposed
Congress, 44, 161 ; influence on
foreign policy, 47, 161–2, 164 ;
estimate, 161–2. *See also* Cavour
Hungary, 9, 157

Printed in Great Britain by
Thomas Nelson and Sons Ltd, Edinburgh